Get Smart

A DAILY DOSE OF WISDOM THAT WILL
TRANSFORM HOW YOU
LIVE YOUR LIFE

*Insights for your money,
relationships, heart, and mouth.*

Randall Sanford

Contents

FOREWARD
Scott Landis—Professional Business Coach

There's an often-quoted principal in leadership that says, "you can't lead someone where you haven't been". I'm not sure who originally said that, but it has stuck with me over the years. It is that principal that has driven me to always be a learner. One thing those closest to me know about me is, I tend to get obsessed about a certain topic or genre, and then research it until I get bored of the topic. Whether it be leadership principles, quantum physics, sales funnels, psychology, bio-hacking, or the latest tech gear, I have probably wasted copious amounts of time "researching important information".

Of course, some of that knowledge stuck, and even less of it was applicable to helping me coach and lead people. But when it comes to knowledge and research which will always be relevant, WISDOM will never go out of style. Taking the time to increase wisdom will have a high ROI every time!

I'm talking about the kind of wisdom that provides the foundation for action in life. Not whatever the latest trend is, or hot topic of the day. The stuff that is time-tested over the centuries. The principles that are as predictable and reliable as gravity. When you learn this kind of wisdom, and apply it, ultimately you can't fail.

So as a leader, you can't give what you don't have. And if you don't have wisdom, there's no excuse because it's out there. In fact, it's in your hands right now. This book is full of all of the wisdom you need for life, love, and leadership. It's worthy of being read and re-read over and over.

One thing effective people do is read something good every morning. This book is perfect for that purpose. This one daily habit will make you more effective at life and more effective at leadership. When you live a life that exudes wisdom, people notice. This makes you more influential. Great leaders are great influencers.

I met Randall in 2012. We were both part of launching CEO roundtable forum organization. Since then we have found ourselves working together under multiple companies and organizations. Until finally, we actually launched our own organization called 360 Leadership Forums. And our flagship offer is a culture-changing curriculum we teach and coach to our clients called Influential.

One of the things Randall and I do, is teach leaders how to lead like coaches. This book is FULL of material that will help you think that way. And it will help you lead others towards fulfillment. What we teach is all about creating a coaching-culture in your organization or team. We've found that leadership from a coaching perspective is the most effective method for creating a culture your employees never want to leave because it is high accountability and high positive regard for the people. It helps your team get personally engaged by aligning their goals and values with that of the business. This book is full of the wisdom required to have that kind of Influential culture.

Why does culture matter? Because businesses with good cultures are more profitable and thriving. At the same time, they are more enjoyable to lead and to work for. So as an executive, when you read this book it will not only help your business thrive, it will help YOU thrive and isn't that what we all want?

INTRODUCTION

WHY DOES IT MATTER?

*W*e are living in the Age of Knowledge, where billions of bits of information, much of it even true, are available at a second's notice.

We are also living in a Confessional Age where each person has the opportunity to "update" the world on how they feel at any given moment. We feel with, commiserate with or celebrate how celebrities that we have never met, feel about the most trivial matters.

There was a time when people's feelings were considered too personal to share with anyone outside their closest family and dearest friends. Few would ever consider exposing their innermost life to strangers. Decisions, even the most seemingly intimate ones, like who to marry, were decided on the basis of what was practical, what "made sense" rather than on more ethereal issues like feelings of love or care. Emotions were confined to the personal, not the public realm.

Not any more!

Now, feelings are everywhere. A noted celebrity in his 40's, found himself on a televised talk show and, letting the world know how much he loved his new girlfriend, made a fool of himself jumping on and down on the studio sofa while telling the world "I love her!...I love her!"

It seems like every decision these days is an emotional one. Many people don't buy a car or home because its the right price or gets good gas mileage, but because of how it makes them feel.

Advertisers and marketers rely on passion driven consumerism.

Even the discussion of the social issues of the day, especially on television and radio, has to be infused with huge doses of ranting and raving emotion in order to be "interesting".

Dispassionate discussion of policy and practice is considered too boring to even all on TV.

On the other hand, we love "the facts". Billions and billions of dollars are spent on research to find new knowledge. The capacity of mankind to do what was once unthinkable (things like cloning or space travel) is exploding as our information database increases at a phenomenal rate. As humans, we know exponentially more than has ever been known in this world's history and that knowledge is increasingly available to us all.

There are college classes on line now, for free, that a few years ago were exclusively available to the most gifted and fortunate students.

Yet in this emphasis on how we feel and what we know, we're missing something important. We forget that our feelings can lead us astray. No matter how much it's said, "trust your feelings", we all know that they can't always be trusted. Our feelings have been proven wrong time and again.

Yet facts are, in some ways, stupid things. Information, by itself, can never tell us what we ought to do. We may have a map but we still would not know if we should take a trip.

Pure knowledge is information without insight. It tells us what is without telling us what we should or shouldn't do with this information.

Albert Einstein said; "Since the advent of the Nuclear Age, everything has changed but the way people think, thus, we drift towards unparalleled catastrophe."

What is missing in all of this is wisdom. Wisdom is the insight to know how to channel and respond to our feelings. Wisdom is the ability to understand the significance of facts and information and how they should, or shouldn't influence our lives.

What we need is a good mentor. Someone who is very wise and can share principles of wisdom with us to guide our lives.

However, it is not enough to have just anyone guiding us. If we were wanting to learn to snowboard, the 16 year old next door could

probably teach us the basics. If our goal, however, is to be in the next Winter Olympics, then we would want to seek out an World Class coach. We would someone who had the knowledge and experience necessary to make us champions.

If the goal is simply to learn to play piano there are plenty of teachers on Craigslist who could get us started. However, if the goal is to be in the Cliburn International Amateur Piano Competition we would need to hire a renowned piano tutor.

Far, far more important than the greatest sports or artistic accomplishments is learning how to live a wise and good life for ourselves and those closest to us. The greatest goal for all of us is true happiness and fulfillment. The desire for which drives us to accomplishment, making money, achieving our dreams. Yet, if our pursuits in life are not guided by wisdom, we may do great things but

never reach our deeper goals. We may be successful but not satisfied.

There are way too many stories of those who have gained riches, become famous or accomplished great things but have ended up completely unhappy and unfulfilled because of the unwise choices they made along the way.

So who will mentor us in this most important endeavor, the pursuit of wisdom? Should we ask the guy next door who is always Tweeting, the woman at work, or the commentators on TV? It makes much more sense, given the gravity of our pursuit, to look to the greatest world class mentor on this subject of wisdom, the wisest person who ever lived; Solomon son of David. And, he's available!

What a privilege we have to learn from him.

God asked Solomon what he wanted. He could have asked for riches or fame or for generations of blessing for his family. After all, it was God Himself who was asking. What he asked for was wisdom.

God granted his request and, we are told, he was so wise that the glitterati of nations heard of his reputation for wisdom and came to simply hear what he had to say.

The Queen of Sheba came 1500 miles (a long way in those days) just to see how Solomon would answer her questions. She was amazed and said, "Your wisdom and prosperity exceed the fame of which I heard."

Solomon penned the book of biblical book of Proverbs and I wrote this book so that we could learn to live successful, prosperous lives as Solomon promises (Proverbs 3:13-18).

Still, as it is with any mentoring relationship, it will take effort and commitment. We will have to read and learn these important principles and get them into our hearts and minds. More importantly, and more difficultly, as we learn what it means to live wisely, we will have to be willing to change in areas of our lives.

This kind of wisdom is not simply something to learn and know, it is a way of life to be lived. We must choose to pursue wisdom. It won't come to us if we don't go looking for it.

So, I am going to ask you, the reader, to make a commitment over these next 40 Days. I ask you to read at least 1 chapter a day (they're short—it won't take you long) and, more importantly, spend some time thinking about applying what you have read.

Get a Bible (or find it online at www.biblegateway.com) and read through Proverbs at the same time you are reading this book. Write down what you are learning as you go along. It will really help you begin to live its principles in your life.

I am asking you to focus on this for 40 days.

In the Bible, we discover that there is significance to this period of time. Jesus fasted for 40 days, the rain storm in Noah's time was 40 days, Moses was with God for 40 days when he received the 10 Commandments, and Jesus showed Himself for 40 days after the resurrection.

Psychologists and counselors tell us that 40 days is a length of time that can produce lasting change in our habits--good or bad. My hope is that in the next 40 days, as you study this book and the book of Proverbs, there will be lasting change in your life, family and other relationships.

I was 13 years old in 8th grade when God gave me an assignment. He told me, "study the book of Proverbs and underline ever scripture that tells you what wisdom is and how to get a hold of it." For the next many months, I read 10 chapters a day from Proverbs. I did my level best to put into practice what it told me about being wise.

Even though I was at that awkward junior high age, even though I hadn't been exposed to a great number of wise and influential people, and I didn't have a lot of knowledge about the world, after that study, person after person commented on how wise I was for my age.

The study of wisdom from the book Proverbs changed me and gave me a life-long love for the pursuit of wisdom. It can do the same for you if you make the commitment and put in the effort.
May God bless you as you do.

Get Smart

What is this thing "wisdom" that we are going to be studying over these next 40 days?

This first section will help us to understand the characteristics of it, why it matters and what will happen if we pursue it.

Wisdom is within your reach—if you will reach out for it. If wisdom, as Proverbs promises, is worth far more than gold or rubies, then your time will be well invested.

Let's get the adventure started!

Get Smart

Section 1

SMART LIVING

Day 1

The Nature of Wisdom

Listen as wisdom calls out!
Hear as understanding raises her voice!
Choose my instruction rather than silver,
and knowledge over pure gold.
For wisdom is far more valuable than rubies.
"I love all who love me.
Those who search for me will surely find me."
Proverbs 8:1,10-11,17 (NLT)

*T*oday we begin an adventure—an adventure in discovering wisdom. We are trained to believe that the wise are like the Marines—the few, the proud, the wise.

But Proverbs makes it abundantly clear that wisdom is offered for anyone who really wants it. In the scripture above, the personification of wisdom is seen as calling out, raising her voice, and crying aloud. She, wisdom, tells us that if we search for her we "will surely find" her.

On the other hand, this is not all automatic.

Voltaire said, "Common sense is not common". The fact is, truly wise people are rare. Not, as we see above, because wisdom is not available, but because we do not take the steps necessary to lay hold of it.

Here are some of the actions that "wisdom" asks us to take in Proverbs 8; "listen", "hear", "choose my instruction". This is exactly what we have set ourselves to do over these next 40 days, to give ourselves over to hearing, understanding and applying the wisdom available to us.

If this study is going to really make a difference in our lives, then we must do more than simply read a book, we have to be willing to change the way we live.

To "listen" means to give the advice you will receive its proper weight. After all it's from God! To truly "hear" means to accept that the wisdom is for our life, and that it applies to us, personally.

Don't make the mistake of assuming that these wise insights are just for the other guy—they are for each of us, individually! To follow the command to "choose my instruction" means to put it into practice, perhaps in place of other earth bound wisdom you have been living out. It means to truly make it a part of how you live.

What will happen if we do? Wisdom makes some great promises. She offers, "Let me give you understanding."

Every one of us in this complicated world, in relationships, in our jobs, just trying to make ends meet, often feel at a loss for understanding. Wisdom promises to give it to us.

She tells us that it is worth more than gold, than silver, than rubies. She promises "riches, honor, wealth and justice."No wonder she can say, "Nothing you desire can be compared with (me)."

So, are you ready? All you have to lose is your foolishness, and there is so much to gain. Let's go on an adventure together and discover how to be wise, how to make our lives really work and see if we are not changed by it.

Day 1 Action Steps

1. Set a certain time each day that you can commit to your pursuit of wisdom (reading in this book, reading in Proverbs, writing down what you are learning). Decide on a time and place where you won't be disturbed and can be consistent.

2. Make a commitment to yourself to be willing to change as you are challenged by the principles you are learning.

Day 2

Who Needs Wisdom Anyway?

These proverbs will make the simpleminded clever.
They will give knowledge and purpose to young people.
Let those who are wise listen to these
proverbs and become even wiser.
And let those who understand receive guidance by
exploring the depth of meaning in these proverb,
Proverbs 1:4-6a (NLT)

Maybe you are asking yourself; "Is this something I need? Will I really benefit from studying the wisdom in Proverbs?" This passage gives us the answer. It tells us that "These proverbs will make the simpleminded clever."

No one I know wants to admit to being simple or simpleminded. The word here means, "pertaining to persons that are easily deceived or persuaded".

Maybe, in some ways, we are all simple...

> Ever have a time when you were deceived or too easily persuaded in a relationship or a financial decision?

> Ever purchased something you regretted later because you were talked into it?

> Ever found yourself in a friendship that you should have avoided?

We probably have all done all of these. We are all need to learn how to be more "clever" in these areas. This cleverness is a quality that wisdom provides.

The insights of this book promise to give young people "knowledge and purpose".

If you are beginning your life as an adult, they are two things you simply must acquire. You may be getting the finest college education or tracing a steep learning curve in your job, but education or training alone will never give you a purpose for your life or grant knowledge of the most important things in life—Proverbs will.

Maybe you consider yourself fairly wise. I am sure many of us do. The danger is that we might miss out on some new truths because we feel like we already have it down.

Someone once made this obvious observation; "You don't know what you don't know." Or as the former Secretary of Defense, Don Rumsfeld said, "There are unknown, unknowns." So, even if you consider yourself wise, come on this journey and perhaps you will discover some wisdom you didn't even know you were missing! Only the fool believes that they have nothing to learn.

Proverbs promises us "guidance". In the increasingly complicated world in which we live, we all need guidance.

Not that there isn't a lot out there. There are guidance columns in the newspaper and a million "experts" on TV or the internet offering you their wisdom. How much better, on the other hand, it is to get our guidance from the one who made us! Solomon wrote the book of Proverbs but God is the one who gave him the insight.

If you want to know how to operate your Chevy van it is surely the best idea to ask the folks at General Motors. How much more should we look to our creator for His guidance as He revealed it through Solomon? He made us, He knows how our lives can best work.

Let's go on a journey of discovery to find out how God would tell us to "operate" our lives.

Day 2 Action Steps

1. List one situation in your life that you need a "wisdom" insight on;

   _____

2. Make a commitment now to watch for the wise insight when it comes along and put it into practice.

Day 3

Happy Are The Wise?

Happy is the person who finds wisdom
and gains understanding.
She offers you life in her right hand,
and riches and honor in her left.
She will guide you down delightful paths;
all her ways are satisfying.
Wisdom is a tree of life to those who embrace her;
happy are those who hold her tightly.
Proverbs 3:13,16-18 (NLT)

Who among us is not looking for happiness? It is so important that the United States of America wrote it into their Declaration of Independence. We Americans, they declared, have the right, among other things, to the "pursuit of happiness." The writers of this declaration put it right up there in value with life and liberty.

These three values were worth fighting a war over.

On the other hand, how many people really find true happiness? The poet Amy Lowell speaks for too many when she writes,

> *Happiness: We rarely feel it.*
>
> *I would buy it, beg it, steal it,*
>
> *Pay in coins of dripping blood*
>
> *For this one transcendent good.*

We are now more able than ever to find something that will give us temporary happiness. In fact our world is filled with pleasure seeking and entertainment, yet the goal for many is simply to be able to forget that they are not happy.

Entertainment, in fact, seldom brings much happiness, but it may bring some distraction from the emptiness too many people feel.

Get Smart

Proverbs promises that happiness, satisfaction, full life and delight will be found by those who gain wisdom.

Perhaps you are asking, "Why should wisdom be the path to happiness and satisfaction? I've heard that it is better to be 'fat, stupid and happy!'"

It's true that many people believe that the less you know, the more happy you will be. They think being blissfully unaware of the world around them will keep them from anxiety, stress and depression.

Unfortunately, the world has a way of pressing itself in on us. We cannot avoid it, even if we wanted to. What we must know is how to deal with it.

Beyond that, wisdom is more than simply knowing the facts. Wisdom is the ability to perceive the world, and your life, with new eyes—to see both for what they really are.

Wisdom, then, is not in the business of teaching us how to better pursue happiness directly, but how to live life so that happiness is the inevitable result.

Albert Camus wrote: "You will never be happy if you continue to search for what happiness consists of."

But, as we study over these next few weeks, as you apply the principles of wisdom to your family, to your pursuit of money, to your relationships, and to how you talk, happiness will find you!

My friend Jimi had lived quite a life; played bass with the great guitarist Jimi Hendrix and made tons of money. Jimi's life, however, was anything but happy and fulfilled. When I met him, his marriage, his family and his life was falling apart.

Jimi changed his life and began to pursue a different way of living--a life of wisdom. He learned how to have a good marriage, how to invest his life in the things that really count, so today Jimi has a great family and is giving himself to care for others. He's happy and he is writing books that are helping people deal with the race problem in our country.

That is the power of a life lived in wisdom.

Day 3 Action Steps

1. What is one area in your life where you are unhappy (your marriage, your money, your friendships etc.)?

   _____

2. Look for and apply the wisdom you discover to this area.

Day 4

How to Get It

Don't turn your back on wisdom, for she will protect you.
Love her, and she will guard you.
If you prize wisdom, she will exalt you.
Embrace her and she will honor you.
Carry out my instructions; don't forsake them.
Guard them, for they will lead you to a fulfilled life.
Proverbs 4:6-8,12-13 (NLT)

*I*f you persist in reading this book, you will discover God's wisdom for your life.

Not because I, as the author, am so insightful, but because the author of the Bible, God Himself, knows everything about the humans He created. We will be discovering His wisdom. The question is, once you have found it, what will you do with it?

The scripture above says, "Don't turn your back on wisdom." In the original language this phrase meant "to desert" someone or something.

How many people know what wisdom is and understand very well the "right" way to live their life, but then choose to desert it, to turn their back on it? If we remember back to the times we have done the right thing and listened to wisdom, we will understand why the writer here says, *"(Wisdom) will protect you."* When we turn our back on what we know we should be doing and do something else, there are consequences. Wisdom, listened to and followed, not deserted, keeps us safe.

The last sentence of this passage in the NIV says, *"Hold on to instruction, do not let it go; guard it well."*

It doesn't seem like so much warning is necessary. Maybe the writer here is going overboard. Once we have found out the right way to live, why would we want to let go? Why wouldn't we hold on to it with all that we are?

The truth is, people let go of wisdom all the time.

A young man walked into my office. He had become convicted that he was neglecting and verbally abusing his wife. As a result, she was looking for attention from other men. "Peter" said to me, "I don't care how long it takes for her to respond to me, I am going to convince her that I love her and I am the one for her."

Two whole weeks later Peter returned and he was fuming; "Randy, I've had it. I tried for two weeks and she is not responding. I am through with this marriage."

He knew the wise way to act in his marriage, but he turned his back on it. His wife and especially his children suffered for that decision.

He is not alone, many go into marriage with counseling and a commitment to live in a wise and understanding way, yet later, these couples let go of, lose track of, or just quit practicing the wisdom they know, and their marriage suffers.

Many things in your life will try to pry you away from the wisdom you will gain during these next few weeks. We will be tempted to become lazy. It will be all too easy to go back to our old habits. Others will suggest ways of dealing with life that are contrary to God's wisdom and we must be ready to reject them and remember what we've learned.

When we get to the last chapters I will remind you how to hold on to what you have already gained. Yet, even at the beginning we must make a commitment to value, honor and guard the wisdom God will entrust to us.

Jesus himself said, "To him who has will more be given, so be careful how you hear." Do you want to be wise? Then commit now to value and hold on to what you learn.

Day 4: Action Steps

1. Is there some area of wisdom that you gained in the past but now have stopped applying to your life?

   _____

2. What do you need to do to begin to apply this wisdom to your life now? _____

   _____

Day 5

Wise Guy or Fool?

A wise person is hungry for truth,
while the fool feeds on trash.
Proverbs 15:14 (NLT)

Which are you, a wise person or a fool? According to Proverbs, that is a very important question to answer.

Proverbs 3:35 tells us that, "The wise inherit honor, but fools are put to shame." We all want honor instead of shame, but how do we measure up on the wise guy (or gal) vs fool scale?

Here are some ways that we can judge ourselves:

The reference above suggests the question; "What do you feed yourself on?"

This is not referring to physical food, but instead, what we feed our minds. There is certainly no lack of junk food for the mind available to us. Unfortunately, our popular culture thrives on foolish entertainment; embarrassing people, making light of immorality, focusing on the sick and bizarre, honoring those with outward appeal but who are inwardly corrupt.

Much of what is available on television, in music, on the internet and even in written material is not worth our attention.

The fool bathes their mind in this stuff. The wise person seeks what is true instead.

When I use the term "true" it is not in the sense of being nonfiction rather than fiction, but true in the sense that it teaches lessons that contain truth and, therefore, has real value. Fiction, like some of the parables Jesus told, can serve as illustrations that illuminate what is true and real.

Much of this world's entertainment depicts just the opposite. What it presents as reality is simply false; that doing the wrong thing has no consequences, that people are to be used and not valued, that this world and getting more and more "stuff" is all there is.

The Bible advises us to dwell on "What is true and honorable and right. Think about things that are pure and lovely and admirable. Think about things that are excellent and worthy of praise."

That is what a wise person does and what a fool doesn't do.

A national TV commentator asked the other day, "Why do people watch 'Keeping Up With The Kardashians?" I too wanted to know so I posted that very question on Facebook. The best answer, and a very sad one, was that it was like a train wreck, people simply couldn't look away.

I just want to say; "yes we can" and "yes we must!"

Proverbs 12:15 points to another difference between a wise person and a fool: "Fools are headstrong and do what they like; wise people take advice."

There seem to be two kinds of headstrong fools: the quiet kind and the loud kind. Some people are stubborn and don't listen, but they also don't argue either. They just quietly go about doing their own thing no matter what other wise people have said to them.

Others make it very clear that they are not listening to what others suggests. They are the, "if I want your opinion I'll give it to you" kind of people. A wise person, on the other hand, realizes that there is always more to learn. They understand that there is often a nugget of truth in what someone is saying. Even in those situations where some of the advice may be off the mark, wisdom may be found in the rest of what they have to suggest.

Solomon tells us in Proverbs 14:8, "The wise look ahead to see what is coming, but fools deceive themselves."

Are you a self-deceiver?

> The kind of person who is too afraid to find out what is left in their bank account?

> You avoid going to the doctor for fear that he will tell you something you don't want to hear?

The wise want to know the truth—even when it is painful to face. The fool, on the other hand, falls back on magical thinking—telling themselves that if they don't know the facts, somehow reality will magically change. You cannot prepare for the future if are not willing to face it.

Are you a wise person or a fool? You decide that question every single day by the decisions you make.

Day 5: Action Steps

1. How many hours of junk TV, internet or movies do you expose yourself to each week? _____

2. When was the last time someone suggested a change in how you lived your life? _____

   Did you listen and make a change or resist what they had to say? _____

Day 6

I'm Not Interested!

If you become wise, you will be the one to benefit.
If you scorn wisdom, you will be the one to suffer.
Proverbs 9:12 (NLT)

Some people simply don't care to pursue wisdom. For them it simply doesn't seem like it is worth the effort. Perhaps you feel like you are wise enough and really don't have that much more to learn. The truly wise understand that there is much they don't know.

That's why it says in Proverbs 1:5, states emphatically, "Let those who are wise listen to these proverbs and become even wiser."

On the other hand, it would be a good idea to consider the other side. What happens if you ignore wisdom? Is there a downside to not giving it the focus it deserves?

The verse above advises us that the same way that we benefit from discovering wisdom, we will suffer if we ignore it. The wording of this verse is a little misleading. The truth is that you are not the only one to benefit when you pursue wisdom—you family and friends do as well. And when you are stubbornly disinterested in it, it is not only you that suffers.

So many families suffer from foolish parents, so many relationships suffer from foolish friends. If you reject the pursuit of wisdom, you will suffer, but so will a lot of other people.

What are the dangers of "scorning" (to make light of, to devalue) wisdom? In other words, what do I have to lose?

In Proverbs 1:25-28 Madame Wisdom says; "Because you disdained all my counsel, and would have none of my rebuke, I also will laugh at your calamity; when distress and anguish come upon you, then they will call on me, but I will not answer; they will seek me diligently, but they will not find me."

If you ignore wisdom when it is offered to you, when you need it, you will not be able to find it. When the most difficult times of your life hit you, you will not be able to find the help you need.

It is a truth of life that often people make their worst decisions under stress and pressure. Why is this?

Because they did not pursue wisdom when things were going well, they did not get these principles set into their life. So, when they really needed wisdom, they simply didn't have it and couldn't find it or perhaps it was simply too late to change things.

I have a friend who recently suffered a medical calamity. He may not be able to ever work again. While his family is deeply upset about what has happened to him, they also know that he is a wise man who has prepared well for the future.

The financial well being of his family is assured, no matter what happens, because my friend has lived by wise financial principles and the members of his family are the beneficiaries. When we live a wise life, everyone benefits.

Proverbs 1:30 says, "The turning away (*or turning back*) of the simple will slay them, and the complacency of fools will destroy them".

To turn your back on the wisdom you have gained or to be complacent, believing that wisdom is not an important, life long pursuit, will bring destruction in your life. At the time you need it most, wisdom will not be there to save you.

Don't let that happen! Make the pursuit of wisdom a priority for you, and when you have it, don't let it go!

Day 6: Action Steps

1. Is there a piece of wisdom that you once held dear that you are no longer following?_____Are you putting those close to you at risk by doing so? _____

2. It has been six days now. Are you still intent on learning about being wise? _____
   In what way could you be more intentional or disciplined in your approach to it? _____

Day 7

Where It All Starts

The fear of the LORD is the beginning of wisdom,
and knowledge of the Holy One is understanding.
Proverbs 9:10 (NIV)

You may be thinking, "Alright I agree. It is important to pursue wisdom, but where do I start?"

The scripture above gives us a good clue; it is the fear of the Lord that starts us on the track to finding wisdom. There are several reasons why this is true:

First: God created all that is. He understands how the world works. He set into place the laws that govern the seen and the unseen world (among others, physical, moral, spiritual and relational truths).

So, when we fear Him, when we have set our hearts to respect Him, and therefore to obey Him, we make a choice to line up with the principles that make this world, our lives and relationships work.

For example, God says, "Give and it will be given."

Since He said it, respect, fear for God, if you will, compels me to be a giving, generous person with my money, my heart and my life. What we discover as we begin to give with generosity is that it is indeed the wisest way to live! Life simply works better that way.

God knows- He is the one who put those principles into the universe!

Second, fear of the Lord not only compels me to listen to what He says for me to do, but also what *not* to do.

There are at least two reasons not to go against God's law.

Certainly it is simply immoral to do what the Ruler of the Universe has told us not to do. Beyond the priority of obedience, it is, practically speaking, in our best interest to obey. Disobedience inevitably releases a destructive force in our lives.

For example, God says, "Do not commit adultery."

I counseled with a married woman who started a friendship with another man on the internet. She knew it was getting out of hand. She knew it could be trouble when she gave him permission to met her. She went ahead anyway and had one sexual encounter with him.

What was the result?

Her husband felt horribly betrayed and eventually divorced her. Their kids suffered, she suffered, it cost the family thousands of dollars and buckets of tears all because she thought she could get away with ignoring God's law. It is never a wise thing to do.

So the fear of the Lord is the beginning of wisdom because it demands that I stay away from harmful and foolish activities that have the potential to destroy me.

Third, as it says in Proverbs 2:6,7a, "For the LORD grants wisdom! From his mouth come knowledge and understanding. He grants a treasure of good sense to the godly."

There probably have been, and will be, many times in all of our lives when we simply don't know what to do.

This scripture tells us that God wants to give us the wisdom we need at those times.

Yet, if we don't respect Him, fear Him, we will not be looking to Him for this wisdom. James encourages us; if you lack wisdom, ask God— He will give it to you! It will be out of a respect for Him, a fear of Him, that we humble ourselves and ask.

All of this brings us to an important issue; How is *your* personal relationship with God? It is impossible to fear or respect someone you don't even know. If you want to be wise, you must get to know, personally, the source of all wisdom, God Himself. The best part is that He wants to be known by you. He wants to help you with the confusing issues of your life.

To know Him requires three things of us: that we humble ourselves, recognize our need for Him and reach out to Him. To find out more about knowing God, look at the end of this book for steps to begin a relationship with the wisest being in the universe. You can start right now by simply asking Him to reveal Himself to you.

He wants to get to know you, why don't you let Him and let Him grant you more wisdom than you could ever imagine.

Day 7: Action Steps

1. Evaluate your relationship with God. Do you know Him, fear Him, respect Him? Describe it here:

   _____

   _____

2. What would you like this relationship to be like?

   _____

   Ask God for the grace to have that become a reality in your life. Reach out for Him and He will reach back for you.

Section 2

SMART MOUTH

Day 8

The Worth of a Word

A person's words can be life-giving water;
words of true wisdom are as refreshing as a bubbling brook.
Proverbs 18:4 (NLB)

This section will teach us wisdom on using our words. Our words have incredible power, both in our lives and in the lives of others.

With that kind of power, it is essential that we discover how to use our mouths to bring about good instead of hurt and damage.

Too many people's mouths are like a toddler with a shotgun. It is not that they have evil intentions, they just do not understand the power they have in their hands and, consequently, that they are a danger to themselves and others. The book of James says of the tongue, "It is a restless evil, full of deadly poison."

Yet, it simply doesn't have to be that way. If we choose to, we can use our words for good and hold them back from evil. That is why it is so important that we understand the wisdom God has for us in using our mouths the right way.

The scripture above points out what we can do in other's lives by using our tongues well. God clues us in on an important piece of wisdom when He reminds us that our words "can be life-giving water".

What does water do for us?

It refreshes, it brings health, it cleanses the outside and the inside. Water can even be the difference between life and death if you have gone long enough without it.

So what about your words? Do they refresh the people around you? When someone hears what you have to say to them, do they go away more whole or more sick? When you talk are people cleansed or dirtied by their interaction with you and your mouth?

Throughout this next section we will be looking at the wisdom Proverbs offers for using and controlling our mouths, and we will discover more and more the truth of Proverbs 20:15, "Wise speech is rarer and more valuable than gold and rubies."

Such a verse seems like an overstatement, but when we realize that our words control our destiny, impact our friends, and bless or curse our marriages and children, then we begin to understand the true value of wise speech.

Wouldn't you love to feel like this verse applied to the way you used your mouth: "Everyone enjoys a fitting reply; it is wonderful to say the right thing at the right time!"

When we learn to speak wisely, certainly our family and friends will benefit greatly, but we will benefit as well.

There is no better feeling than to know that you have made a difference in another's life, that you have encouraged them just when they needed it, or that you have given them counsel that really made a difference.

I had a friend and colleague, Rich, who was this kind of encourager. He found the best in people and called it out. He often said, "You're the best." Of course not all of these people could have been the objective "best" but Rich saw the "best" in them and let them know.

What was the result? Everyone loved Rich. People stepped out to care and to serve because they knew that Rich believed in them and saw the best in them. And he was happy because he was making a difference with his life and with his mouth.

Let's study and learn to get a "smart mouth" together.

You, as well as everyone around you, will benefit.

Day 8: Action Steps

1. Take the next few days and monitor your words. Watch for the effect they have. Are they a positive or negative force on those around you?

2. What is one thing you should (and will) change about the way you use your mouth?

_____

Day 9

What a Difference a Word Makes!

Words satisfy the soul as food satisfies the stomach;
the right words on a person's lips bring satisfaction.
Those who love to talk will experience the consequences,
for the tongue can kill or nourish life.
Proverbs 18:20-21 (NLT)

What can our words produce in others lives? What effect can what we say have on our families and those we care about the most?

The verses above tell us about one effect our words can have, "Words satisfy the soul". If you have children, think about them for a moment (*my wife and I have 5, so I have a lot to think about!*). What do their "souls" need?

When you were a child, what do you wish your parents would have fed into your soul?

Our words can feed our children's self-esteem. Our words can let them know that they are loved and cared for. Our words can paint a picture of a positive future for them. It is health food for our kids' souls.

It is not just our kids, our friends' souls will also benefit from the same kind of diet. We all need to be told that we are doing well, or that someone cares about us and thinks highly of us. When we satisfy others' souls, we are helping them to be all they can be.

"The tongue can kill or nourish life." Have you ever seen someone who is fed on a diet of discouraging, damaging words, perhaps from a parent or a spouse?

You can literally see the death in their eyes. The spark of life, the hope, the positive expectation we all need goes out, killed by another's words.

My friend Dave grew up in a family with three sons.

His two brothers went through school, did well and went on to pursue successful, professional careers. Dave, on the other hand, is an artist, something his parents never really understood. Instead of encouraging and praising his artistic bent, they criticized him for not being more like his brothers.

Because of how his parents used their words to discourage instead of encourage Dave, he had a very hard time getting started in life. It was difficult to figure out what he wanted to do and harder to get started in it. He had no confidence. He lacked initiative and so much of it was simply lacking the verbal affirmation he needed from his Mom and Dad.

Proverbs 12:18 brings it home very clearly, "Some people make cutting remarks, but the words of the wise bring healing". Think about the words you have spoken even today, or over the last week.

Are they cutting remarks that wound, or wise words that bring healing? You may not be a doctor or nurse; you may not be able to bring physical health to others, but you do have the power to heal their souls—if you are careful about how you use your words.

For example, Proverbs 12:25 says, "Worry weighs a person down; an encouraging word cheers a person up."

So many people around us are drowning in worry about the future. We have the ability to help relieve them from the suffering that this worry brings.

All it takes is something that costs us so little and yet is so valuable to them—an encouraging word from us. It is something we all can give.

It requires just two things from us: first, the willingness to be aware of when it is needed and second, the initiative to speak it out. Our words can do a world of good if we are simply willing.

One of the greatest accomplishment of our lives would be to learn how to use our mouths wisely, to be a part of God's work of bringing healing and wholeness to other's lives.

Day 9: Action Steps

1. Think of someone; it may be a friend or even your
   spouse or child, who needs some encouragement today.
   Call them, write them, talk to them--let them know that
   someone cares and thinks highly of them.

2. Is there anyone in your life that you have been
   discouraging by the way you talk to them? List their
   name and make plans now to contact them, apologize
   and make it right.

_____

Day 10

A Dangerous Mouth

Fools get into constant quarrels;
they are asking for a beating.
The mouths of fools are their ruin;
their lips get them into trouble.
What dainty morsels rumors are—
but they sink deep into one's heart.
Proverbs 18:6-8 (NLT)

As we saw in the last chapter, what we say can bring blessing and encouragement into people's lives.

On the other hand, we have to understand that our words also have the power to bring what can only be described as a curse, a curse on others or even on our own life. As the verse above shows, our quarrelsome mouths can result in conflicts. It may not be that we will get into literal fisticuffs because of the wrong word, although that has been known to happen. More likely, our untamed tongue ends up stirring up conflict, even with those we love.

Have you ever wondered in the midst of a conflict, "How did this fight even start?"

Too often fights can start because we are all too ready to talk about how others get on our nerves, treat us unfairly, or what needs to change for our comfort and selfish happiness.

Proverbs 17:14 gives some good advice; "Beginning a quarrel is like opening a floodgate, so drop the matter before a dispute breaks out."

This constant desire to push for our own way is what our first scripture calls "quarrels". It warns that the result of this quarreling is a "beating".

Again, it may not be that someone will take us out and physically beat us up, but if we have a quarrelsome attitude towards life, life beats us up. People avoid us, relationships fracture and the things and people that matter most to us will be lost.

Our son Samuel has some special challenges in his life. He was born with Downs Syndrome and later diagnosed with both ADHD and Asperger's Syndrome.

It is probably not too hard to guess that Samuel has a hard time controlling his mouth.

His mouth gets him in frequent conflict with his parents, sister and teachers at school. He is told over and over, "stop repeating", "those are not the kind of words we use in our home", "no one wants to hear you talk like that", "don't yell at your sister" etc.. Still he persists.

My wife Gloria and I constantly work with him and challenge him in this area because we know that what comes out of his mouth will have a great influence on his life, his success and relationships. We are all too aware that if we are going to prepare him for life, we must help him get his mouth under control.

For all of us, if we want to learn how to live wisely, we must learn to look for agreement instead of something to argue about. Find every bit of what another is saying that you can agree with, and let them know. This will make your relationships stronger rather than weakening them.

By the way, they will listen to us more once they know that we have first listened to them and found points of agreement.

Proverbs 11:9a certainly should catch our attention. "Evil words destroy one's friends". We might not think that our words are "evil". Perhaps we just feel like we're passing on some small juicy tidbit of information. We don't think that it will hurt anybody.

But the scripture for today makes the nature of rumors and gossip so clear—"they sink deep into ones heart."

Or, as Proverbs 16:28 says, "Gossip separates the best of friends"

When we gossip, we may tell ourselves that our friend will never hear what we have said about them. The truth is, they will and it will hurt, deeply. The next time you are about to say something negative about your friend or enemy ask yourself, "If they were here, would I say it?"

If the answer is "no" then understand this; they will hear about it, and what they hear is very likely to be worse than what you said.

We must learn to use our words wisely. They have the power to destroy us, to destroy others and to destroy our relationships.

Let's be wise enough not to let this happen

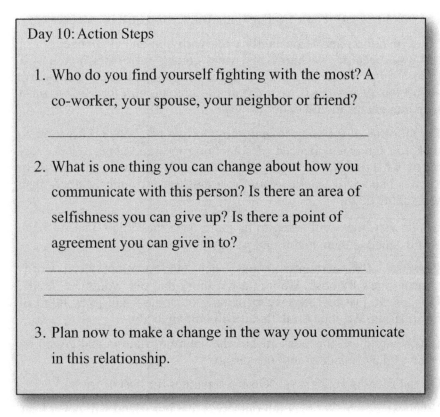

Day 10: Action Steps

1. Who do you find yourself fighting with the most? A co-worker, your spouse, your neighbor or friend?

   _____

2. What is one thing you can change about how you communicate with this person? Is there an area of selfishness you can give up? Is there a point of agreement you can give in to?

   _____

   _____

3. Plan now to make a change in the way you communicate in this relationship.

Day 11

First the Heart—Then the Mouth

The mouth of the righteous brings forth wisdom,
but a perverse tongue will be cut out.
The lips of the righteous know what is fitting,
but the mouth of the wicked only what is perverse.
Proverbs 10:31-32 (NIV)

When our mouths get out of control it is not really a mouth problem, it is a heart problem.

Jesus told us in Matthew 15:18, "But those things which proceed from out of the mouth come from the heart".

The mouth that shares true wisdom with others is one connected to a good heart. So when we discover that our mouth is doing damage, the place to focus is not our mouths but about a foot lower—in our hearts.

All the discipline in the world is not going to help if our hearts are not changed first.

So let's take a look under the hood—let's see what is inside that might be motivating our speech.

Here is what Jesus warned us to look for in our hearts: "From the heart come evil thoughts, murder, adultery, all other sexual immorality, theft, lying, and slander." (Matthew 15:19 NLT)

How do you show that you hate another person in your heart? By how you talk about them.

If in your heart you have given space to lust and sexual fantasy, the way you talk, no matter how carefully you try to hide it, will sooner or later reflect it. If you have told yourself a self-serving lie enough times on the inside, it will come out of your mouth as though it was the true even if you know better.

In 2010 Rep. Mark Kirk, who was running for the US Senate from Illinois, got himself into some trouble by making a false and repeated claim that he was named the Navy Intelligence Officer of the Year in the late 1990's.

He also said, "I commanded the war room in the Pentagon" which also turned out to be false. He had simply told himself a lie enough times that it inevitably began to come out in his speeches.

So what do we do? How do we change our habits, and how do we change our hearts? It is important to say this; what will *not* work is summed up in this one word, "reformation". No matter how hard we try to reform our actions, it will simply not work. Because that is not where the problem is, it is much deeper than our actions. It is our hearts that are the issue.

The good news is Jesus came to earth not to reform people, but to transform them from the inside out.

Proverbs 16:23 tells us, "From a wise mind comes wise speech". But our minds will never be wise if our hearts are corrupt. God's goal is to change our hearts and transform our souls.

This in turn will change our ways of thinking and, as a result, our ways of talking.

Do you desire to change? You can't do it by yourself. Only God can truly change us. Here is your part: humble yourself right now as you are reading this and ask God to forgive, cleanse and change your heart. This will bring about the needed transformation in your mind and mouth.

As God transforms us from the inside out, we can fulfill the promise of Proverbs 10:31; "The godly person gives wise advice".

As our personal transformation effects the way we use our words, we are able to pass on true wisdom that will make a difference in other's lives as well.

Day 11: Action Steps

1. Take some time to answer this question; What do your
   words reveal about your heart, good or bad?

   _____

   _____

2. If you haven't done so yet, ask God for his power and
   grace to change your heart. He is the only one who can.

Day 12

Don't Be Dumb!

A lying tongue hates those it crushes,
And a flattering mouth works ruin.
Proverbs 26:28 (NASB)

There are some very unwise ways that we can use our words. Today we will look at some practical principles to keep us from tripping over our own tongues.

Our opening verse is a great place to start. We sometimes tell ourselves that when we lie to another person it is for his or her good, or at least it's neutral. We think to ourselves, "This little white lie won't hurt them, and it will keep me out of trouble".

Yet when we lie, we do hurt the other person, even, as this scripture suggests, when we are flattering them—telling them a good lie to make them feel better.

Everyone operates most wisely in life by knowing the truth.

When we lie we are giving false information that will harm, not help the listener. That is not to suggest so called "brutal honesty" all the time.

We will look tomorrow at the many proverbs that suggest we keep our mouths shut—and that is often a good idea. If, however, we do speak, we must tell the truth. Do it in love, but tell the truth.

When we care enough about others to tell them the truth, even if it is to our disadvantage, we allow them the possibility to make wise decisions.

For example, you and your friend Jane get together for coffee. Jane is a Wonder Woman, tremendously competent and able, but really lacks people skills; empathy, tact and understanding of others.

She tells you that she is contemplating leaving her current job for a new one. However, in this new job she will be supervising others and will need to have be very good at handling people.

She asks for your input. "Am I taking the right step? Do you think this is the right move for me?"

If you flatter her, telling her that "you will do just fine", even if that is what she desperately wants to hear, you are not helping. You are in reality hurting Jane. She is likely to end up in a job that she will fail at, and you will be part of the reason she does.

Another mistake we make is complimenting ourselves. Proverbs 27:2 reminds us, "Don't praise yourself; let others do it!" In fact, when we praise ourselves, others usually won't. They don't want to encourage our pride. We should be careful with boasting about what we've done or what we have. It turns others off and makes them feel like we are competing with them.

Here is another area to watch out for; we need to be careful about giving others advice.

Proverbs 18:13 gives us these guidelines on giving advice, "What a shame, what a folly, to give advice before listening to all the facts." And Proverbs 18:17 tells us, "Any story sounds true until someone sets the record straight."

What then is wisdom for the advice giver?

Don't answer the *"What do I do now?"* question too quickly. Make sure you know all the facts first and, at times, if pertinent information involves another person, get their perspective before you answer. It is the wise thing to do.

So many times when I have begun to do marriage coaching with a couple, one of them will come to me first and tell me everything that is wrong with their mate and why the whole marriage problem is their fault.

I have discovered the wisdom of saying, "You know, I can't really fix them, they are not even here. Let's talk about what you can do better first and see where that leads us. Next week all three of us can talk together"

Inevitably, when the spouse shows up the next time, there is more to the story than I initially heard.

It is simply wisdom to withhold judgment until we hear the other side of the story.

Our tongues can be used wisely or foolishly. Let's learn how to employ our mouths in the service of wisdom.

Day 12: Action Steps

1. Who around you needs to know the truth? Not a hurtful truth but information they need to know that you have been withholding to protect yourself. Plan now to start being honest with them.

2. Do a self evaluation; Do you talk about yourself too much? Do you brag about what you have or have done? If you answered yes to either of these, make a commitment now to change your ways and begin being humble in how you communicate.

Day 13

Turn Off The Flow

A truly wise person uses few words;
a person with understanding is even-tempered.
Even fools are thought to be wise when they keep silent;
when they keep their mouths shut, they seem intelligent.
Proverbs 17:27-28 (NLT)

*H*ere is a story that illustrates how our tongue can get away from us.

A young man was on his first day on the job. He was a new clerk in

the produce department of a super market. A lady came up to him and said she wanted to buy half a head of lettuce.

He tried to dissuade her from that goal, but she persisted.

Finally he said, "I'll have to go back and talk to the manager". He went to the rear of the store to find his supervisor, not noticing that the woman was walking right behind him. When he got into the back of the store, he said to the manager, "There's some stupid old bag out there that wants to buy half a head of lettuce. What should I tell her?"

Seeing the horrified look on the face of the manager, he turned around and, seeing the woman, added, "And this nice lady wants to buy the other half of the head of lettuce. Will it be all right?" Considerably relieved, the manager said, "That would be fine."

Later in the day, he congratulated the boy on his quick thinking. He then asked, "Where are you from, son?" The boy said, "I'm from Toronto, Canada, the home of beautiful hockey players and ugly women."

The manager looked at him and said, "My wife is from Toronto." The boy said, "Oh, what team did she play for?"

Maybe you have felt that way at times. Proverbs 21:23 admonishes us, "Watching what you say can save you a lot of trouble". It is very true and very important to remember.

When you read all that Proverbs has to say about keeping our mouths shut ("keep silent", "don't talk too much", "turn off the flow", "use few words", etc.) we might begin to get the impression that what wisdom dictates is that we never utter a thought. Maybe it is wisest to always keep it all to ourselves.

That is really not the point of these admonitions.

The wisdom God is offering is to learn to think before we speak. Even more, *listen* before we speak. Really listen to what others are saying, not just on the surface. What are they communicating, however unclearly, from their hearts? The wise person learns to read expressions, body language and tone to get the whole picture before they respond.

Not only should we really listen to others, but we must learn to listen to God before we speak. Often He will tell us when it is time to speak, and when it is time to remain silent. But He can only do that if we take the time to hear the "still small voice".

If we are going to be wise in how and when we speak, it is crucial that we slow down enough to listen to others, to our own hearts and minds, and most importantly to God.

Day 13: Action Steps

1. Monitor the words that come out of your mouth over the next 24 hours. Take note of the times when you could have done just as well or even better by saying less.

2. Take time today to really listen to a significant person in your life, a parent, spouse, child, a dear friend and try to see what more you can pick up by listening with focus and engaging all of your senses. Practice turning off the "I need to say something back" response and just concentrate on them and what they are saying.

Day 14:

Your Mouth and Your God

The Lord hates those who don't keep their word,
but he delights in those who do.
Proverbs 12:22 (NLT)

How we use our mouth is not just an issue for ourselves and those around us, it is also an issue between us and God. As this verse makes clear, He really does care if we live up to the promises we make with our words.

The CEV translates the second part of this verse like this; "God is the friend of all who can be trusted".

Do you want to be a friend of God? Then make sure that when you promise something, you do it.

We make promises all the time. Our biggest problem is that we make them too lightly.

We promise our children to do something for them or with them, or we tell our friends that they can count on us. Then we proceed to break those promises too easily because we made them to lightly.

We must learn to really think about what we're saying when we give our word. We must never forget the hurt that we can cause when someone is depending on us and we don't come through—especially our kids. I have sat in my office many times counseling with adults who have carried deep wounds for years because of unkept promises from their parents.

Probably the most significant promises many of us have spoken were on our wedding day. There, with family and friends and in the sight of God, we made solemn vows to love, care for and stay true to our spouses.

We meant every word of it. Every bride and every groom intends to live up to these commitments they make on that day. Unfortunately, many don't.

Get Smart

How about you?

If you are married, do you remember the day you stood and made promises to the one you love? As the years have gone by, has your commitment to love and cherish, and to stay faithful in mind as well as in body begun to weaken?

Remember this; God was a part of that commitment. He watched you make it, and even if you didn't recognize it at the time, He cares intently whether you keep the commitments you made that day.

God hates it when we don't keep our word because He knows the destruction that comes from broken promises and failed commitments.

Today I encourage you to ask Him to give you the power to renew your vows, to recommit yourself to your spouse, and to make a renewed effort to live up to you made when you married them.

Not only does God care about the promises we keep, but He desires that we use our words in partnership with Him, working with Him to accomplish His will on earth. In the Lord's Prayer Jesus told us to pray, "Your will be done on earth as it is in heaven."

Sometimes it seems like prayer is a pretty pointless act—telling God what He already knows. But here we see the real point behind prayer. God gives us the responsibility to call out in prayer His will on this earth.

We have been given the privilege and responsibility to work with God to see His will done. In His wisdom He has determined not to act until we use our words to ask Him to do so.

Do our words in prayer matter? They sure do. They move the hand of God to act.

My friend Char believes strongly in the power of our words when they line up with the will of God. Her son was playing baseball when his arm broke. Everyone there heard it break and Char and her son rushed off to the hospital.

The doctor told them that because of the break her son would need to be in a cast for several weeks. Char knew better. She knew that her son was supposed to pitch in a game the very next weekend and she knew what God's will was and so did her son. Both of them said, "This arm is not broken, it is going to be fine."

As they stood in faith and believed what they heard God say, the pain went away and his arm was healed. He was, indeed, able to pitch the next weekend.

Why did that happen? Not because Char's words have great power in themselves. It happened because her words and her son's words in prayer confirmed the will of God for that situation.

Let's realize the power our words have and use them to see God's will done.

Day 14: Action Steps

1. What is one promise you have made in your life that you have not kept? _____

   _____

   If it is in your power to do it, keep that promise this week.

2. Do you have a promise from God that you need to grab a hold of? Write it down right here:

   _____

   _____

   Agree with God and pray His promise back to Him.
   Do this every day this week.

Section 3

SMART FRIENDSHIPS

Day 15

Friendships that Pass the Test

A friend is always loyal,
and a brother is born to help in time of need.
Proverbs 17:17 (NLT)

*"T*he better part of one's life consists of his friendships."

- AbrahamLincoln.

Friendships can enrich our lives or cause great pain.

They can make us bitter or better. They can be a force for incredible good or terrible evil. In this section we will discover some of the wisdom Proverbs has for us in finding, keeping and interacting with our friends.

We will learn how to pick good friends and what destroys relationships. We will discover how to protect, how to challenge our friends, and how to deal positively with conflict in our friendships.

First, we need to see how valuable friendships can be.

As the proverb above indicates, one of the great values of having a friend is that they are there for you when tough times hit. It is hard enough to go through painful, difficult times. It is many times harder to go through them alone.

As the old saying goes, "Joy shared is double joy; sorrow shared is half sorrow."

We might be tempted to wonder about our own friends and ask, *"Are they loyal, would they stick with me through the hard times?"*

Yet, we should really be asking ourselves;

"Am I a loyal friend or am I only there for the good times?

Am I willing to sit and grieve with my hurting friend when they need it?

Will I give them a shoulder to cry on and spend time with them even when it's not fun?"

That is the essence of true friendship. Aristotle said, "Misfortune shows those who are not really friends."

Recently I have had the occasion to observe this kind of friendship in action. "Jamie's" husband suffered a severe stroke. In fact it was not just one stroke, but several.

He was in the ICU for weeks and she rarely left his side. Every time I would go to visit this family, Jamie's friend Sue was right there supporting her, encouraging her, bring her food, books to read and games to play.

She was the one who took over the job of communicating to the rest of their circle of friends how things were going and how to pray. She picked up their kids from the airport, and took them back again. She made sure that they didn't have too many visitors, or too few.

In the midst of this tragedy, Sue was a true, loyal friend.

Proverbs 19:22 relates these words of wisdom; "What a man desires is unfailing love". There is not a human being alive today who does not crave "unfailing love." The word used here means unrelenting kindness and devotion.

This world seems intent on destroying our sense of worth and value. Our bosses tell us we're not doing enough or not doing it well enough. Circumstances contrive to make us feel like losers. Something inside looks for just one person, our friend, who will see the value and worth that seems to hide from the rest of the world and call it out of us.

Unfailing love is not easy to maintain precisely because it is *unfailing*. All of us place conditions on our love.

We want to love at all times, but when our friend says or does the wrong thing, we withdraw our love out of hurt or pain.

Proverbs 27:10 tells us, "Never abandon a friend, either yours or your father's".

I am not suggesting that we should allow someone to abuse or destroy us or for us to pretend that it is not happening. I *am* suggesting the mindset advised by Proverbs, to begin with a commitment to be a faithful friend.

In the next few chapters we will learn the wisdom of confronting and how to do it, but the place to begin is with a foundation of unconditional love.

Day 15: Action Steps

1. Think of a 2-3 of your best friends. Are there any of these that you have not been in contact with lately?
   _____ Give them a call. Write them a text. Send them an email. Reach out and reconnect.

2. Who do you know that is going through a tough time right now?_____Contact them and see how you can help, even if it is as simple as an encouraging word.

Day 16

A Little Caution Goes a Long Ways

A man of many friends comes to ruin,
But there is a friend who sticks closer than a brother.
Proverbs 18:24 (NASB)

*F*riendships can be wonderful!

They can add to your life and make it better— even make you a better person. On the other hand, Proverbs 22:26 advises us to be "cautious in friendship".

If friendships are so wonderful, why is it necessary to be so careful? There are two good reasons.

The first is expressed in this Latin saying; "It is as bad to have too many friends as no friends at all."

When we begin to build friendships we make certain commitments, explicit or implicit, to that friend. Things like being available to them in hard times, spending quality time together or prioritizing them into our busy lives.

These kinds of commitments are impossible to keep when you have too many friends. What inevitably happens is our friendships become "a mile wide and an inch deep." There is little time to spend with each one and, consequently, not much intimacy, understanding or care.

The flower of friendship grows best in the soil of time together. We only have so much of ourselves, and if we divide our attention, priority and focus among too many people, we will be doing all of them a disservice, not to mention the rest of our life's priorities.

So how many are too many friends?

There are a lot of factors that go into answering that question. Things such as family responsibilities, the demands of your job, or how much free time you have all make a difference.

Experts say that for most people it is hard to maintain more than 5 or 6 close friendships. For those who have a lot of other responsibilities, even 3 or 4 may be too many.

The reason for this is not to restrict friendships, but to make sure that these vital relationships have the chance to fulfill their greatest potential in our lives and in those of our friends.

"Rick" was a man who loved people. He loved people so much that he had, truthfully, more than one hundred close friends. He told them that sincerely and repeatedly; "you are such a good friend." The problem was that Rick was constantly frustrating them. As can be imagined, he had little time to spend with any of them and, when he did, it was usually in a group setting.

That was not very satisfying to his "dear" friends.

I was one of those friends. I worked with "Rick".

He asked me out to lunch one day and I was looking forward to a chance to talk to him about some personal issues. He showed up at my office ready to go . . . with three of his other friends who I didn't know very well.

Rick says in front of them, "I hope you don't mind if they come with us." Of course I minded and I didn't handle it very well. I told him that I had hoped it would be just the two of us in front of his embarrassed friends.

Unfortunately, this kind of thing happened often in Rick's life. In fact, I am convinced that one real reason he left the place where we worked together was precisely because he was being burned out by trying to deal with the needs of all of his friends.

The second reason we should be "cautious in friendship" is found in Proverbs 22:24-25; "Make no friendship with an angry man, and with a furious man do not go, lest you learn his ways and set a snare for your soul."

Just like teenagers, we will become like those we hang around with, and not just in the area of anger.

Whatever weakness a person is dealing with, they will have a tendency to pass it on. That is not to say that your should desert your friend if they recognize that they have a problem and want to change.

No, rather the writer here in Proverbs is commenting on the person who is not willing to change, who is content in their weakness. If you continue to be friends with a person like that, you are putting yourself at risk of becoming like them.

Friends are supposed to influence others. Friends are supposed to be an example for each other. If you have a friend who is influencing you the wrong way, get out of the relationship.

You can't do them any good if you are being pulled astray. Make sure that God and living as a godly person are always first—even before your friendships.

Day 16: Action Steps

1. Take an inventory: Do you have at least one good friend?

   _____ Do you have too many close friends
   (probably more than 4-5)? _____

   What are you going to do with this insight?

   _____

2. Do you have a friend or friends that are

   leading you astray? ____

   If so, how can you turn this around, either by

   influencing them or getting out of the relationship?

   _____

Day 17

Lose Lips Sink Friendships

Scoundrels hunt for scandal;
their words are a destructive blaze.
A troublemaker plants seeds of strife;
gossip separates the best of friends.
Proverbs 16:27-28 (NLT)

The scripture above points out the wisdom of being careful with our words when it comes to our friends. Our friendships can be made stronger or destroyed by what we allow out of our mouths. In the last section on our words, we looked at how unwise it is to gossip. Since it is a particular struggle that many people deal with, it bears at least this much repeating—if you want to be wise, don't gossip!

Still, there is more to learn about how our words can impact our friends.

The verse above starts by making it clear that it is not the best kind of person who looks for scandal. In fact, it calls them "scoundrels"--a worthless person, lacking in value. It doesn't speak too well of the person who loves scandal.

That is a tough piece of wisdom for us in modern day America. As a society, we love scandal. Careers have been started on it. Whole industries are built on reporting the latest, smallest detail of the hottest current gossip about the most popular celebrities—and most of us are caught up in the gossip.

So what's wrong with having an "inquiring mind"? What could possibly be wrong with intently following the latest divorce or court case of our favorite (or least favorite) celebrities?

The problem is that it gives us a taste for scandal. We get a thrill when we feel like we know something others don't—even if we are one of a million viewers of that show that night. Having tasted that thrill, the power of having inside information, it is so much easier to pass on what you have learned about your friend. It feels the same as all the other times when you discussed other scandals in the lives of people you didn't know.

Once you allow yourself to take joy in another's downfall, it is very difficult to draw the line with your friend's problems and failures. You will find yourself talking about it just like you did about the movie star's latest divorce. So start by making a wise commitment to refuse to find enjoyment in the failures and difficulties of others, famous or not.

The scripture we started with tells us that a "troublemaker sows seeds of strife." If we are not careful, our friendships themselves can be a launching place for strife. It can start when we simply share how we have been hurt by another person.

Naturally, we want to have others understand us and commiserate with what we have gone through. However, if we are not careful, the outcome is division and broken relationships.

Too often, what we are really saying is, "Either you are on my side or against me—on 'their' side."

We draw lines and make our friends choose. This is sowing seeds of strife and it is destructive to others and, ultimately, to your friendship. Our goal, especially as Christian brothers and sisters, should be unity and never division.

I was the pastor of a church when we encountered a theological controversy. Some thought that our worship should be more free and expressive and others thought that we were alienating the more conservative members of the congregation and pushing away visitors from our community.

This discussion could have been good and healthy. The congregation and leadership needed to figure out what kind of worship style we would promote. The problem was that too many took sides and forced their friends to stand with them or against them. Because of this strife the whole church became divided and its purpose, helping people grow and reaching out to others, got lost in the disagreement.

In the end, it was a tragedy for everyone simply because individuals wanted others on their "side" more than they wanted unity for the whole.

We cannot let our friendships become the garden where seeds of division grow.

Day 17: Action Steps

1. Do you love scandal?_____How much time do you spend reading about it or watching reports about it? _____ If you need to, how can you change this?

   _____

2. Have any of your friendships become a venue for creating strife and division? _____
   How can you change this? _____

   _____

Day 18

The Wisdom of Encouragement

Two are better than one,
Because they have a good reward for their labor.
For if they fall, one will lift up his companion.
But woe to him who is alone when he falls,
For he has no one to help him up.
Ecclesiastes 4:9-10 (NKJV)

We are put together with our friends not just for mutual enjoyment but to help each other. We all want and need someone who will lift us up when we fall down, but what is *our* commitment?

Are we aware of those times when our friends are down and discouraged so that we can lift them up? That is part of what encouragement is all about, friends bound together in heart who will not let the other give up. We all need to be reminded from time to time that God is working a larger plan in our lives than we can see at the moment. When our friends loses a job, their marriage is in trouble, when they are facing the hardships of life, they need us first, simply to be there with them in their pain.

Because we are there at the right moment, with the right heart, we have the opportunity to remind them, when they are ready to hear it, that God's plan is always for their good and not for their destruction; that He always is working something great out in their life.

It is one thing to know this truth, it is another to walk this faith walk with a friend by our side.

I have a friend who went through a very difficult time with his business. Some months it looked like he was not going to be able to pay his staff. There were times when he even wondered if he would have to declare bankruptcy.

I remember riding in his car one day as he drove to the mailbox wondering if enough money would come in the mail to keep his company going for another week.

65

He was literally shaking as we drove.

As best I could I let him know that I cared about him and what he was going through—that I loved him. I had no idea how to advise him on his business, but after assuring him of my love and commitment, I did my best to help him to believe that God was going to bring good things out of the hard times. I knew that God had put me there to encourage my friend.

Later I went through the darkest time in my life. People who said they loved me turned their backs on me and caused me, my family and the church I pastored great pain and grief. At that point my friend returned the favor—he was there for me.

He allowed me to vent my feelings without judgment. He loved me even when I was unlovely, and then he reminded me that God still had good plans for me. I could not have made it through those dark days without his support. Such is the power of encouragement.

Ecclesiastes 4:12 says, "Though one may be overpowered by another, two can withstand him."

Encouragement binds us together, and together we are stronger. There will be things in our lives that we simply cannot face alone. That is why God has given us friends—but we need to ask for the help.

Women many times are better than men at this. They, less often, let their pride get in the way. But all of us, men and women, need to remember to ask! How can those around us know that we need them unless we ask them?

Sometimes the strength we need to get though comes simply by asking our friends for support.

It could make a world of difference.

Day 18: Action Steps

1. Do you need support right now? _____
   Which of your friends will you call to ask for help?

   _____

2. Do you have a friend who needs a word of encouragement?
   _____ Contact them today and give it to them.

Day 19

The Wisdom of Encouragement
Part II

You will keep your friends if you forgive them,
but you will lose your friends
if you keep talking about what they did wrong.
Proverbs 17:9

I like what Oliver Wendell Holmes said, "Except in cases of necessity, which are rare, leave your friend to learn unpleasant things from his enemies; they are ready enough to tell them." Another translation of the first part of the verse above says, "He who covers an offense promotes love".

In the next couple of chapters we will be talking about how to confront and deal with conflict, because confrontation and conflict are a part of wise friendships.

Before we turn that corner there is wisdom in considering what to overlook rather than confront. The gracious art of overlooking another's faults gives space for them to become a different person.

There are two ways that we can help bring change in our friends' lives. The first is confrontation; challenging them to grow and pressing them to face their faults.

The second way is the path of acceptance and encouragement; to look beyond their faults and recognize the potential they have to become more than they are.

It is when we see that potential and relate to them on the basis of what they can become, rather that what they are <u>not</u>, that change is encouraged.

Henry Ford said, "My best friend is the one who brings out the best in me." Or read what Goethe wrote; "Treat people as though they were what they ought to be and you help them to become what they are capable of becoming."

Every one of us has someone greater inside of us just waiting to be born. The encouragement between friends helps to make this potential a reality. We need to realize the power that our position has in the other person's life. If we know that someone truly cares, then we listen and believe what they have to say about us.

Because of this, friends have great power for bringing out the best in each other.

It is with eyes of faith that we see what our friends can become, the same way God does with us. He is always saying, "I know you can do better. I see you as perfect and right." Can we, should we, do less with our friends?

We must be willing to see beyond their faults to what would happen if their weaknesses no longer limited the strengths God created them with.

As friends, we can remind them of those strengths.

In 1980 I was working at a church in Hermosa Beach California. I was six months into a one year internship as the printer for the church, as well as leading the Single's Group.

One day my pastor pulled me aside and said, "We have decided to hire a full time Single's Pastor. The rest of the staff wanted another guy *(who I saw as very good looking, talented and several years older)* but I told them that you were the guy. I know you can do a great job."

This was a leader who I respected and admired. I appreciated him as a mentor and friend and when he said that I could do this job, suddenly there was no doubt in my mind, I could do it.

His confidence and belief in me, even though I was just 21, gave me confidence in myself.

For all of us, it all comes back to the power of the tongue. What are you using yours for? Give those closest to you a vision of what they can be and the hope that they can live up to that vision.

Day 19: Action Steps

1. Do you talk to others about your friends' failures, or do you help them overcome those failures? _____

2. Who can you talk to this week who needs you to see the best in them and call it out? _____

   When will you contact them? _____

Day 20

A Loving Rebuke

A truly good friend will openly correct you.
You can trust a friend who corrects you,
but kisses from an enemy are nothing but lies.
Proverbs 27:5-6 (CEV)

*Y*esterday we learned about the wisdom of seeing the best in people and even choosing not to expose their faults.

Today we read that being corrected by a friend is a good thing! In fact, we learn it should inspire us to trust them.

So before we learn more about "a loving rebuke", we need to know when to cover over faults and when to confront them. Proverbs 27:17 tells us "As iron sharpens iron, a friend sharpens a friend."

This verse suggests that part of the answer is understanding when a loving rebuke will make our friends better (when it will sharpen the blade) and when it would simply discourage them from wanting to change (when it will dull it).

If we take the time to be sensitive to our friend's moods and place in life, we will have some understanding of when a correction can be tolerated. Too often we base the passion of our rebuke on how *we* feel, rather than on how our friend is prepared to deal with it.

We also must consider their personality.

For example, I am most motivated by a straightforward, straight out challenge to change. It is vital that I realize (finally) that many people are not like me.

Many others are terribly crushed by such an approach. They honestly feel like they are trying their best to be the best, and to hear that they are failing is a crushing blow. For these kinds of people, gentle encouragement is usually the best approach.

Having said all of that, we need to remember how valuable a clear word of correction can be.

Many of us work hard to keep others from pointing out our faults even though that is not the way of wisdom.

We need to know what we are doing wrong so that we can change for the good. The wise person will realize that most people avoid confrontation at all costs. Our friends really would rather not take the risk to tell us where we need to grow. So, when someone does offer correction, or when we are brave enough to share it with our friend for their good, it is a good thing.

I remember the day clearly. I thought I was a pretty relational guy. I was a Single's Pastor and led a group of nearly 200 singles. My friends had a different idea. Cathy and Wendy came to me and said, "We feel like you are too isolated. It seems like you really don't have any intimate friends."

At first I was mad but then I began to think about what they said. They were right and as I committed to changing the way I lived my life and pursued relationships I became a better pastor and better person.

I'm sure it wasn't easy for them to confront me. I was not only their friend, but their pastor as well. Yet, it was worth it. It made a huge difference in my life.

Proverbs 17:10 says, "A rebuke impresses a man of discernment more than a hundred lashes a fool."

A rebuke should impress us if we are a person of discernment. If the weaknesses in our lives are changed as a result of this correction we will avoid a world of hurt. The discerning person understands how great a positive impact confrontation can have in their life.

If your friend challenges your behavior, even if comes across lacking in the requisite love and understanding, learn from it and grow. The process of dealing with criticism has been compared to chewing gum. When we are criticized, chew on it until you get all of the flavor (truth) out of it and then spit it out. It is wise to avoid both tendencies;

to reject correction out of hand and risk missing something we need to learn, or to take to heart false criticism and be devastated by it.

So, if we see a weakness in our friend that will result in greater strength if confronted, we should love them enough to talk to them.

If you take the time you will be glad you did in the long run.

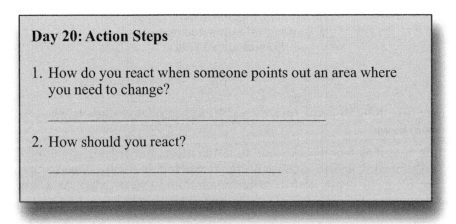

Day 20: Action Steps

1. How do you react when someone points out an area where you need to change?

_____

2. How should you react?

_____

Day 21

Friendly Conflict

It is to a man's honor to avoid strife,
but every fool is quick to quarrel.
Proverbs 20:3 (NIV)

The first thing to know regarding conflicts in relationships is when to avoid them.

It is a curious fact that we tend to not confront our friends when they really need it and to argue with them when it is totally unnecessary. The place to begin with conflict resolution is the wisdom to know how to not let conflicts begin in the first place.

As the scripture above suggests, much of what we argue over could very well be left unsaid.

How many friendships are destroyed simply because one of the parties, or both, can't leave a sore subject alone?

It becomes a point of contention that ruins the good feelings between them. Some issues simply don't matter between friends.

For example, if one is conservative in their politics and the other liberal, do they really have to try to convince each other of the correctness of their position? Will it do any good?

There is a much greater likelihood that it will cause unnecessary damage.

I was counseling with a young man recently. He recounted a argument he just had with his friend.

It was all about the end of times, the Rapture and the Mayan Calendar. It lasted from 2:00 to 6:00 in the morning! There was a great deal of lost sleep, maybe some hurt feelings but no change in belief and, certainly, no change in attitude or action. What a waste!

However, there are two kinds of issues that have to be confronted in a relationship. One is if the behavior of your friend is destructive to themselves or to those around them. In that situation you owe it to them to let them know what you are seeing.

The second is when they are acting in such a way that is truly injurious to the friendship and threatening the continuation of the relationship.

When either of these situations exist, we have to act. We can't just let the relationship slip way. We owe it to the friendship to step up and say something.

When we do confront it is not out of a desire to "tell them off" or to "get it off of my chest". The only right motivation for confrontation is for *their good*—not ours. It should be as difficult for us to say what we have to say as it is for them to hear it.

I remember my first "pastoral" confrontation. A couple who had been in the Single's Group for some time were planning to get married. I had learned that they were living together and because we had all agreed that co-habiting was not right, I knew I had to talk to them about it.

I never prayed so hard. I went with fear and trembling.

I certainly did not want to do it, but I know I had to.

I met the guy at his work. We were able to have a few moments privately. I told him what I had heard and why I was concerned. He confirmed the accuracy of the report and immediately committed to making things right.

I discovered that day not only the power in confrontation for good, but also that it did not have to be as scary as I thought it was going to be.

Jesus gave us some very practical pointers for dealing with confrontation; "If a fellow believer hurts you, go and tell him--work it out between the two of you. If he listens, you've made a friend."

Wisely, He tells us to go by ourselves and talk to them. That suggests a couple of things we should not do.

First, don't talk to someone else about what your friend has done to you. Talk to the friend first.

Second, we may fear the confrontation, we may be concerned about the other's reaction, but be brave and go alone. We can't take along others to "lend support" and underline to our friend how right *we* are.

Dealing with it one on one makes it easier for them to admit their error and change without feeling like everyone knows what they did.

When someone is confronted by a group of people, the natural tendency is to offer a defense rather than really listening to what is being said.

Do you want to deal with conflict well? Learn to see the situation from the other person's perspective--see it through their eyes. Work to understand how they feel. Take time to learn about their background, their personality and their temperament. Listen to learn, rather than talk so much.

As it says in the book of James; "Be quick to hear, slow to speak and slow to become angry".

The more you understand, the less unnecessary conflict you will have and the better your friendships will be.

Day 21: Action Steps

1. Is there anyone who you need to confront right now? _____
   Is the issue important enough to require a confrontation? _____

   Is your heart right as you approach this (in other words, will you speak out of anger or love and concern)? _____

2. If the answer is "yes" to the two last questions, when are you going to talk to them? _____
   Remember to make sure it is in private, just between the two of you.

Section 4

SMART FAMILIES

Day 22:

Families That Stand

*The wicked perish and are gone, but
the children of the godly stand firm.*
Proverbs 12:7 (NLT)

As I said before, I have five children, so I have learned a little, sometimes the hard way, about parenting. I want them each to be successful, independent adults someday.

As parents we all want to believe that our children will do well long after they have left our homes. We have not succeeded as parents if our kids only do well when they are under our care. The real test is how they do when they are on their own.

Parents try to teach their children all kinds of important things—how to manage money, how to get a good job, the importance of education etc. Too many parents forget how important it is to teach their kids to live a godly life.

Perhaps as you are reading this you are thinking; "That is just what a pastor is going to say—'it's important to teach your kids to be godly'. I agree, but is there any practical value in it? I want them to be more than just goody-goodies, I want them to excel and live a good and happy life."

The wisdom of the opening scripture is that being godly and being successful go hand in hand. What is it that causes most kids to fail at their educational pursuits? Isn't it drugs, alcohol, sexual entanglements, the wrong kinds of friends or basic bad attitudes?

These are the very things that "godly" kids will stay away from. Not because they have to be forced to, but because it is in their hearts to stay away.

What kinds of employees are sought after? Aren't the hard-working, honest ones who put others first? Those are the very values that godly people live out. That is because learning to be godly *is* a success-oriented strategy.

One way to help our kids be more godly is to teach them from a young age, as my parents did, that we will always do our best to do the right thing, all the time. We choose to do the right thing not because of fear of the law or because we might get in trouble, but because we don't want to offend God. Stealing, cheating, hurting others is wrong because God says so.

Still, teaching them the rules is not enough. If they are going to be godly, it will be because God is inside them, working on them to become more like Him.

Our kids need a *personal* relationship with God. Godly kids come from godly parents who are not afraid to talk about their relationship with God or to pray with their kids.

Encourage them to read the Bible on their own as soon as they are able. Make going to church a regular part of family life. Ask them about their relationship with God—often.

Later this week we will deal with the value of learning from our elders. If we are going to be an "elder" worth learning from, we need to be an example to our children in how we love people, live life, talk to and about others and in our commitment to sexual purity.

My son deals with both Autism and Down Syndrome. There are so many wonderful things about my son Sam. He is funny, he is enthusiastic, but what he is not, is obedient. He will not come when I call him. Unfortunately, I find myself raising my voice to get him to come upstairs or out of his room.

As I have gotten older, I have found it harder and harder to run after him and lead him by the hand out of these places. The down side is that I find myself yelling for him and then getting upset with him because he is yelling. I tell myself that raising my voice is a reasonable accommodation to the situation at hand and Sam's yelling is just unnecessary, rebellious and obnoxious.

He doesn't see the difference.

If I want him to change, I have to change first and serve as his example.

We have to take seriously our responsibility to be godly examples if we wish to raise godly kids who can stand firm their whole lives.

Day 22: Action Steps

1. What change(s) do you want to see in your child(ren)'s life? _____

2. Are you an example of the right kind of behavior in this area? _____
   If not, what do you need to change? _____

Day 23

The Worth of a Wife

Find a good spouse, you find a good life--
and even more: the favor of GOD!
Proverbs 18:22 MSG

A report in a recent issue of Forbes magazine reinforces this piece of wisdom.

"Economists say that marriage is good for you. Married people are healthier, both physically and psychologically; they live longer; they benefit from a kind of all-purpose insurance policy against adverse life events.

Married people earn more money. They are also happier, citing survey data not just in the U.S. but in the European Union, Russia and Latin America. It's true for both men and women."

The problem too often, for too many, is that we don't recognize this value. It is too easy to point out what irritates us about our spouse, what we don't like or what we wish was different.

We fall into comparisons; "Why can't my wife be like her". "My husband could really learn from him."

The truth is, we all have things about our marriages we wish could be different, but all of us also have glaring imperfections ourselves. It is all part of being human.

However, it is just as true that the vast majority of us, whether we recognize it or not, are greatly benefited by having the husbands or wives that God has graciously given us.

Since we have been graced by God with a great life partner, what should we do?

First, thank God for them. Something very powerful happens when we express thanks regularly for the person He has given us to be married to. We begin to see the good instead of just the bad in them.

Their shortcomings, in our eyes, decrease and their strengths increase.

When was the last time you told God how thankful you were for the very valuable husband or wife that He gave you? Start today and do it every day.

The second thing we all should be doing is telling our spouses how much we value and love them. It is far too easy to get into the habit of constant criticism—always seeing what is wrong and needing to be changed.

What is the ratio of compliments to complaints in your marriage? Dr. John Gottman from the University of Washington has discovered through extensive research that "in functional marriages there are five times as many positive interactions as negative interactions. This ratio of five to one can predict whether the couple has a stable marriage or is headed for divorce."

When you express thankfulness to your spouse and act in ways that show you are glad to be married to them, you are building up this ratio. Because of this positive ratio, when the inevitable difficult times of conflict come, you have a reservoir of good feelings to draw upon.

Even if you think your spouse is not a great source of good in your life, you still have the chance to be a blessing to them by how you treat them. Everyone has some qualities that are praiseworthy and valuable. Thank God for them and point them out often to your spouse.

If you start encouraging the best in them, they will begin to be the person you would like them to be.

Day 23: Action Steps

1. What is one thing that bugs you about your husband or wife (don't write it down)? Can you consciously choose to fully accept them and love them in spite of this?

2. What is one great thing about your spouse? Write it here:

   _____

   Tell them, more than once, how much you appreciate this quality of theirs.

Day 24

Semper Fidelis

Be happy with the wife you married when you were young. . .
you should be attracted to her and stay deeply in love.
Don't go crazy over a woman
who is unfaithful to her own husband!
Proverbs 5:19-20 CEV

If you are a wise person, you will be a faithful husband or wife.

Unfaithfulness in marriage is stupid, costly and dangerous but, in our

sex soaked society, it is all too common. Infidelity happens nearly twice as often with men than with women. Many feel like they are justified in cheating because they are missing out on something important in their lives. They feel like their wives simply are not enough of something; not sexy enough, not young enough, not supportive enough.

Solomon captures this disenchantment so well in the scripture above and challenges us to remember why we married our wives in the first place. It is a choice that we can make to be happy with them.

As it said in the last chapter, the place to begin is by thanking God every day for our wives; "Thank you Lord for a wife who loves me, and is committed to me."

Beyond that, become a student of her and find things that are worth complimenting and tell her about them. Love is not just a feeling, it is also an action.

Choose to serve your wife and you will find that you love her even more. Act in loving ways and you will find that your feelings follow. We may not always be aware that this is true, but we love those we serve. The more we serve from the depths of our hearts, the more we love.

The other half of the equation deals with "the other woman". Proverbs 6:25 advises us, "Don't lust for her beauty. Don't let her coyness seduce you".

As wise and faithful husbands, we must guard three gates to our souls to avoid being drawn into an illicit relationship.

The first gate is our eyes. It is that second look, that choosing to give place to sexual attraction that will get us into trouble. We live in a world that is awash in pornography, and when we choose to indulge ourselves in it, we learn to look at women with disrespect; as mere sexual objects existing for our pleasure.

This makes it harder to look away when we should. Stay away from pornography and avoid the second glance.

The second gate we must guard is the gate of our hearts. Early in Proverbs we are charged, "Keep your heart with all diligence".

It is when we are taken by another woman's beauty, her attractiveness, even comparing her to our wives that we allow another barrier to be broken down. You know when that barrier has been breached when you find yourself thinking of this other woman all the time, and wondering what a relationship with her would be like.

Pastor Jack Hayford in his excellent book The Anatomy of Seduction, relates a personal story about an assault on that second gate of his heart. Early in his marriage he was working near a woman he found himself attracted to. He writes about the mental preoccupation that came along with the illicit attraction; about how he would arrange for her to be invited to meetings, reasoning in his own mind that since she was such a help to him, she needed to be there. His real motivation was to make possible a conversation after the meeting.

Eventually Pastor Jack realized the trap that was set for him and how he was walking right into it. He saw that his heart was being drawn away from his wife, causing him to blow her minor flaws out of proportion. He began to forget his commitment to faithfulness to her.

Fortunately he stopped in time before any physical contact took place. He made the changes necessary to insure that he would not encounter this woman again.

He did what he had to close that gate to his heart.

After the gates of the eyes and the heart has been breached, the third and final gate is the gate of seduction. For most men the greatest seduction is the woman who gives him that sensual look, tells him how wonderful he is and builds up his bruised ego.

The man who has let this woman into his mind and heart begins to believe that she can meet needs his wife never could or will.

It is then the final barrier is crossed and he gives in to acting on his feelings, and the affair begins.

Proverbs says of those who have transgressed this line; "He destroys his own soul. Wounds and disgrace are his lot".

Don't let it happen to you. Be wise—fight your battles at the entrance of the first two gates so you won't have to deal with the third.

Protect yourself, your marriage and your family.

Day 24: Action Steps

1. Men, how is the purity of your heart in sexual matters? (think about it, don't write it down) Have you let down your guard at either of the first two gates? What are you going to do to change that? Do you need some help? Then get it. Find a group or individual counselor who can help you. Write me at randall@vision2lead.coach for suggestions.

2. Have you lost control of the third gate? Are you being unfaithful to your wife? What are going to do to get free from this entanglement? Again, find a group, get a Christian counselor, write me but do something now before your life is destroyed.

Day 25

Wise Wives

The wise woman builds her house,
but with her own hands the foolish one tears hers down.
Proverbs 14:1 (NIV)

How does the foolish wife tear down her own home?

One thing that this book of wisdom warns wives about, more than anything else, is the tendency to be contentious and complaining. For instance Proverbs 21:19 says, "It is better to live alone in the desert than with a crabby, complaining wife."

One way that a wife and mother can be destructive to the health of her home is by not watching her own attitude.

God gave women a keen sense of what is wrong and needs fixing in her family. She is the first to be aware when one of the children is having a hard time or going astray. She has a special sense as to when the marriage, or her husband, needs special attention. This is definitely true in our home! Gloria, my wife, is just like this.

The danger is that when a wife utilizes this awareness and seeks resolution to these situations, she can become negative, nagging and contentious.

The question for wise wives and mothers is "how do you engage in solving these problems without tearing down the family—treat the cancer without killing the patient?"

First, just like the men were admonished in the last chapter, wives too need to cultivate thankfulness.

Husbands and kids want and need to know that they are appreciated for who they are and what they do *now*, even before they change. They need this even more than being told that mom understands their struggles and wants to help them in their weak areas.

They usually know where they are weak. They sometimes wonder if anyone notices where they are strong and able.

Being specifically thankful for their good qualities will create an appreciation of them and help them be ready to work for their own change and growth.

Remember that ratio of five positive interactions for every negative? When there are a lot of problems that need to be addressed and dealt with, there will be a need for even more positive input to keep things balanced.

Second, timing is crucial. Everyone has those times when they are open to correction and input, and other times when they just "don't want to hear it".

Gloria and I have twins, a boy and a girl, who are 14 years old at the time I write this. Even though they are twins and the same age, their talk-to-me schedule is very different.

This is most apparent after school. As soon as my daughter gets home, or even on the way home, Sarah loves to tell about the day's drama; who is friends with whom and who is no longer friends with whom. She shares about her classes and the challenges they represent.

Sam, on the other hand, has only one thing on his mind when he returns from school; basketball!

When he gets off the bus he runs into the garage and grabs his ball and starts playing in the driveway. His time to share, if he shares at all, is after he eats or just before going to sleep as mom holds him.

So, as a wife and mother, you must become a student of your husband's and kid's cycles.

As with our Sam, Dr. Dobson has pointed out that kids are often most receptive just before they go to bed.

On the other hand, that may not be the best time for your husband. Try to avoid the times when they are most stressed, irritable or even hungry. When they are feeling relaxed and satiated, they are more likely to listen.

Thirdly, many of the scriptures that depict the wrong way to deal with problems compare it to dripping water. We all know the irritation when we can't get the sink to turn off and it just keeps dripping until it drives us crazy. It is the same way when a wife or mother (or dad, or father) continues to "harp" on a problem without letting up.

It is wiser to present your concerns in a few sentences (especially with your kids) and then give them time to deal with it, and give yourself time to pray for them.

Children do not respond well to speeches (This is a tough lesson for a pastor, we love to preach at work or at home!). In fact, after just a few minutes they are hearing very little of what is being said.

So, to deal with an issue, find a good time and keep it short. You will get more change, faster change and better results.

Day 25: Action Steps

1. Moms (or dads), when is your children's best time to really talk and receive input from you as a parent?
   _____

2. Take note over the next day or two. What is your ratio of complements/correction toward your husband, toward your kids? _____
   If it is less than 5/1 what can you do to change that?
   _____

Day 26

The Value of Wise Parenting

The father of godly children has cause for joy.
What a pleasure it is to have wise children.
Proverbs 23:24 (NLT)

Our children have the potential to be the greatest sources of joy or of pain or hurt and disappointment in our lives as parents.

In contrast to the verse above, Proverbs 17:21 says, "It is painful to be the parent of a fool." The next chapter will deal with the area of wise discipline—how to discipline our kids according to God's principles.

Consider how valuable it is for our kids to live as they should. As parents we can't control every decision that our children make, especially as they get older. We shouldn't feel as if we must take responsibility for each bad decision they make, but we do have a great deal of influence, especially in the formative years. We must learn to use that influence wisely.

If a godly child is a source of joy, then is stands to reason that we should encourage godliness in our children from a young age.

As I mentioned in the first chapter in this section, kids who have been trained to live morally and to cultivate a clear sense of right and wrong will do much better in the world. Our job is to encourage this godliness in them.

Teach your kids to be wise.

When my older kids were young we studied the book of Proverbs thoroughly. We even took some of the scenarios found in it and acted them out as skits. They loved it, and it was teaching them to be wise. Our twins, even when they were just six years old, were memorizing Proverbs 3.

Gloria and I know how valuable wisdom is, not just as a spiritual value but as a practical one as well.

Proverbs 17:25 says, "There is no joy for the father of a rebel". In my counseling experience, rebellious kids are the number one most painful parenting issue. If you don't want to have your kids grow up to be rebellious, there are three important things you can do as a parent (besides teaching them about godliness).

First, make it a point to be involved with their lives and make it clear to them that you love them—tell them often!

Don't let work or simple busyness get in the way of supporting them. Don't make them act rebelliously break the rules just to get your attention.

Second, be as consistent as possible in disciplining them from the time they are young. Realize that rebellion doesn't simply appear overnight. It is an attitude of heart that begins in childhood. Make it clear from the beginning that disrespectful attitudes will not be tolerated. Be kind but confront rebellion at its earliest stages.

Third, be an example. How often do we as parents act with disrespect in the way we talk about our bosses, our political leaders, police officers, spiritual leaders and others that God has called us to be submitted to.

If you don't want your kids to be rebellious, then show them an example of your own submitted spirit.

Kids can be a joy or a burden, a pleasure or a pain. As parents we need to do all we can do from the start to help them be a blessing to us and to the world around them.

Day 26: Action Steps

1. If you have children what are you doing to train them to be godly and wise?

   _____

2. There are three good parenting goals: to be involved, consistent and an example. Which of these are you strongest in?

   _____

   Which needs some work?

   _____

Day 27

Wise Discipline

Discipline your children while you still have the chance;
indulging them destroys them.
Proverbs 19:18 MSG

There are many reasons that parents are indulgent with their children. Maybe they were forced to do without as a child themselves and, because of it, find it hard to say "no" to their kids. Perhaps they hate confrontation and it is simply too painful to even think of the resulting conflict when they have to restrict their child's wishes.

Maybe they are just lazy and it is easier to say "yes" than "no" and deal with the aftermath. Some parents feel guilty for their lack of involvement in their kids' lives, and being lenient makes them feel better.

No matter the cause, if you are a parent who finds it hard to say no, you need to listen to the wisdom of this verse; You are *destroying* your child.

Because of the lack of parental discipline, your child is likely not to develop self-control. You could be making it harder for them to succeed in relationships, school, or work life. It may even be putting their lives at risk as they may find it hard to say no to risky behaviors like drugs, alcohol or dangerous driving.

The verse above says, *"Discipline your children while you still have the chance"*. The best chance for discipline is when they are young. Don't wait until they are 11, 12 or 13 to start disciplining them. It will be tremendously harder. Begin when they are young and discipline will have the greatest positive effect.

To some sensitive parents, it may hurt them to have to be tough with a 4 or 5 year old. But Proverbs 13:24b talking about children says, "He who loves him is careful to discipline him." Discipline shows love. It is for their best.

The method of discipline is not as important as its consistency. It won't work if we discipline today and let it slide tomorrow. A child, or even a teenager, needs to know that the line between what is allowed or not allowed is always the same and will be consistently enforced.

Proverbs 19:21 gives us another piece of good wisdom; "An inheritance obtained too early in life is not a blessing in the end."

An inheritance is money or things that are not earned but simply given as a gift. In our efforts to bless our kids, to give them the opportunities we didn't have, we must be careful about giving them too much too early.

In the middle class community I live in, some kids in high school have been given $40,000 cars. They have all the latest clothes, electronics or anything else, as soon as it comes out on the market.

What does that teach them about the value of working to earn the things they want?

I am afraid that they are not learning to value what they have. It may very well breed into them a sense of entitlement, "I deserve the best and I shouldn't have to wait for it." This can lead to debt problems, a deep sense of selfishness and a short term "I have to have it now" mentality.

Part of wise discipline is to teach our kids to wait and *earn* the things they want. It won't hurt them to work at home or at a part time job to get the latest and greatest new thing. Gloria and I tried to instill this into our children.

My daughter Rachel learned this lesson and is amazing with money. She and her husband are just in their 20's, she has worked as a school teacher and he is just getting started in his career. In spite of this, they already own rental properties and have paid off all of their student loans way ahead of time.

This success with money was evident early on in her life. She began saving for college when she was ten and making a dollar an hour babysitting. When she got her first car, she could have gone into debt and bought something shiny and new, but she took the little she had and bought a small, high mileage used car that would get her back and forth to college. Later, when she graduated, she again used cash to buy a used car with money she earned while working her way through school.

If, as a wise parent, you help your kids to learn the value of what they have (or want), they will be more careful with it and live life with less of a sense of entitlement.

That is wise parenting.

Day 27: Action Steps

1. Take note of your parenting over these next few days. Are you being consistent in the way you lead, direct and discipline your children? _____
   If the answer is no, where do you need to start building more consistency? _____

   _____

2. Observe your kids. Do they exhibit a sense of entitlement?_____Have you done anything to contribute to that? _____
   What changes do you need to make to ensure that they appreciate what they have? _____

   _____

Get Smart

Section 5

SMART MONEY

Day 28:

The Wise View of Money

Better a little with the fear of the LORD
than great wealth with turmoil.
Proverbs 15:16 (NIV)

*W*hat is money for? Why do we want to have it?

Since so much of our lives are spent in the pursuit of money, we really ought to consider what we are hoping to gain in the pursuit. For most of us, down deep inside, we believe that we will be happier if we have more money.

The truth is, study after study has made it clear that money will not bring happiness.

Recently there was a frenzy over $600 million being up for grabs in one lottery drawing. Everyone was imagining themselves a millionaire and considering what they would do with the money. Maybe they hadn't heard about the study that traced what happened to previous winners and discovered that, on the average, the happiness they found by winning had totally dissipated in one or two years. Many of them experienced significant problems besides.

Many people think that money equals security. We think that if we have enough money then we are insulated from the difficulties of life, that you can be free from worry or anxiety. However, Proverbs 11:28 says; "Trust in your money and down you go! But the godly flourish like leaves in spring."

Reality is the more you have, the more you worry about losing it.

Money can't provide true security because the most significant things that impact our lives negatively; tragedy, illness, loss, and misfortune, arc not things that mere money can protect against.

There is no insurance that will guarantee your future. No one knows what is going to happen tomorrow, and only God can control it.

So, if money can't make you happy or secure, what is it for? The following scriptures provide the alternative and suggest the answer.

One says, "Better is little with the fear of the Lord". The other, "The godly flourish like leaves in the spring". The alternative to trusting in money is trusting in God.

God is the only one who can give you true happiness—what the Bible calls joy. Joy can be defined as having a positive, optimistic outlook on life no matter what happens.

Only God provides the ability not only to endure the difficulties we all face but to have real joy even while we are still in the middle of them. Only God is big enough to provide the security that we all want.

God's Word promises us; "God will meet all your needs". He uses money to meet those needs—at times. Sometimes he provides in other ways, but He always provides for His kids. Because He has made this promise, we can trust Him to give us what we need instead of trusting ourselves. Because He has made this promise, we can be secure. We don't have to worry.

The image of the moment is as clear in my mind as if it happened yesterday, even though it has been nearly 50 years ago. My dad was the pastor of a small church in Nampa, Idaho. He always taught our family and the church that God is our provider and can be counted on to take care of our needs because of His love for us.

I remember when he gathered us together and showed us his wallet. It contained a single dollar bill. That was all the money we had. He showed us this, not to worry us, but so that our whole family, me, my two brothers and my mom, could pray with him believing for God's provision. Even though our family had very little in the way of income, God had provided, over and over and we were certain that He would again.

And indeed, He did. We were in Nampa for three years and even though the church was unable to pay my father, much at all and our family had three hungry growing boys, our needs were always met. We always had enough food to eat and a roof over our heads. I was even able to go to a private kindergarten.

I remember one interesting God provided for us (interesting, at least for me, a 5 year old who wanted to watch my cartoons). My dad started fixing TVs to make a little extra money on the side so even though we couldn't afford to buy ourselves a TV , he brought home a regular steam of them so we always had one to watch. That was just one example of how God showed His loving provision to our young family, even when it didn't involve cash.

It comes down to this; what do you fear, the future or God?

A healthy respect for His power and greatness creates trust that a great God will provide in a great way.

It requires that we do not take ethical shortcuts to provide for our selves.

My challenge to you today is to ask yourself, "Who am I trusting to provide for me and my family; myself or God? What gives me a sense of security, my ability to provide or God's?"

Begin thanking Him today for His provision and going to Him when you have needs. Start trusting Him more and yourself less to give you provision and security—that's being smart.

Day 28: Action Steps

1. What is your greatest fear when it comes to money?
   _____

   What does this reveal about your trust and reliance
   on God to provide for you? _____

2. Spend some time every day this next week thanking God for everything He has given you.

Day 29:

Working Wisely

A little extra sleep, a little more slumber, a little
folding of the hands to rest—
and poverty will pounce on you like a bandit; scarcity will
attack you like an armed robber.
Proverbs 24:33-34 (NLT)

In the last chapter we discovered how God wants us to trust Him and not ourselves for our material provision—to look to Him for security and to provide for our needs.

Someone might be tempted to think, "Great, now I am off the hook. I just get to sit back and watch the stuff roll in. None of me, all of Him. Great God, do your thing—PROVIDE for me!"

However, that is not how it works! Trusting God is more than just waiting on Him to give us stuff. It means that we will do what He tells us to do—that we will be part of His system of provision. Over the next few days we will be looking at what our part is in God's plan.

Do you want to make sure your needs are provided for?

Don't we all want that?

Then let's discover what we must do and learn to do it well.

The first thing God calls us to is to avoid being lazy. God doesn't need our work any more than, as we will discuss later, He needs our giving in order to provide.

The truth is that being diligent instead of lazy is good for us. God loves us too much not to press us to do what is best for us. Lazy people lose the great joy of fully realizing the potential God gave them when He created them. That's why He says in no uncertain terms, "Don't be lazy." If we are going to succeed in life, we have to be willing to do those things that may not be easy or comfortable.

The opening verse for this chapter refers to sleeping too much but for some the equivalent of sleeping too much is watching TV instead of balancing their checkbook. Or, perhaps saying "yes" to another charge on their credit card when you should be saying "no". It may be the unwillingness to work that extra hour that would have made us that prized employee.

We have been educated to find the easy way out of every situation. There is so much stress naturally in the world that we look for comfort and ease when and where we can find it. There is nothing inherently wrong with rest or sleep, and there is nothing inherently wrong with avoiding stress. Where it becomes dangerous is when we know we should be taking action and don't. That is when we risk losing out.

The first part of Proverbs 24:30-34 says, "I walked by the field of a lazy person . . . I saw that it was overgrown with thorns. It was covered by weeds and its walls were broken down. . ."

What is your equivalent to broken walls and overgrown fields? What needs your attention right now in your work, home or family life?

Do you want to be blessed by God in your finances? Take action in that area and don't procrastinate. God will not reward laziness with His provision.

Day 29: Action Steps

1. What has God put on your heart to do? (E.g. go back to school, start a business, get a better job, volunteer in the community)

2. What, if anything, holds you back from doing that?

   What next step can you take in the next few days to begin doing what God has given you to do?

Day 30:

Wise Giving

It is possible to give freely and become more wealthy,
but those who are stingy will lose everything.
The generous prosper and are satisfied;
those who refresh others will themselves be refreshed.
Proverbs 11:24-25 (NLT)

God's word tells us that the "the liberal soul shall be made fat." That is not suggesting that Democrats will gain a lot of weight! What it means is that the person with a liberal soul, a soul that is open and generous, will be rewarded.

There is a belief in our world that if we hang on tightly to all that we have, share as little as possible, pay as little tax as we can, and, of course, not give anything away, then we will prosper.

That is this world's system not God's. In fact, His is just the opposite. If you want to be blessed you need to give. If you want to receive, you have to open your hand to give to others.

There are many places in the Bible where we are commanded to consider the needs of the poor and to give to them.

We may think that providing for such people is the government's job —that if we pay our taxes we have done our part, but God knows that it is good for us to have the compassion and thankfulness that expresses itself in generosity.

Besides being the right thing to do, it has the advantage of also being the wise thing to do. God blesses us when we give to others.

Make it a practice to support those caring for others who have less than you do. Be willing to give to those around you who have found themselves in need of help.

For example, do you have an extra car you don't need?

Perhaps you should consider giving it to someone who needs it. Keep your ears open to the needs around you that you can do something about.

Proverbs tells us, "Honor the LORD with your wealth, with the first-fruits of all your crops; then your barns will be filled to overflowing, and your vats will brim over with new wine."

First-fruits is another word for a "tithe", literally 10%.

If we want to be blessed, if we want our bank accounts to be overflowing, then we are called upon here to tithe. We need to give God the first 10% of what He has blessed us with.

My father, Jerry Sanford, says, "Isn't it great of God that He gives us everything we have and then lets us keep 90% of it." The tithing concept reminds us where our wealth, and everything else we have comes from. The tithe is our way of saying to God, "I recognize that it is all from you and I want to give some back."

Speaking of my father, he is proof that the tithing concept works. For nearly 15 years they worked in small churches making very little but always tithing and giving generously. God blessed them with a new house when most people would have looked on their situation and said, "there is no way they can buy a house," but God provided.

Because they were generous with God and others, God was generous with them. Now, in their retirement, even though they never made a lot of money, they have a summer and winter condo, rental properties and enough resources to be well provided for. Why? Because they gave generously, God has taken care of them generously.

There is a great promise in this verse, "Your barns (*bank account*) will be filled to overflowing and vats will brim over with new wine". If you want to see it happen in your family's finances, think about what it means to honor God with your wealth.

Give to those in need, and if you're not doing so, start tithing and expect more blessing than you know how to handle.

Day 30: Action Steps

1. Do you tithe (give 10% of what you receive to God)? _____
   If not, start. Maybe you are not a believer and don't know
   why you should do anything the Bible says to do. The
   challenge: try it and see if you are not blessed. The Bible's
   principles work for all people, whether they are Christians
   or not.

2. Who do you know that is in need right now? _____
   Plan right now to give them a generous financial gift. It will
   be good for you!

Day 31:

Wise Wealth

The blessing of the Lord makes a person rich,
and he adds no sorrow with it.
Proverbs 10:22 (NLT)

I am convinced that it is not God's purpose for us to "just make it" in life. What He wants for us is bless us with riches. The word "rich" in the passage above means "more than the norm for society", and that is what God wants for us.

Now, let me be clear. I am not saying that if you are not wealthy that you must have done something that has caused you to miss God's blessing. What I believe this verse is saying is that God wants to bless each of His kids, all of us, in a very generous way. It certainly makes it clear that it is not *against* God's plan for any of His children to be wealthy.

God is all for wealth.

The rightness or wrongness of wealth depends on what we use that wealth for. We can use it in ways that honor God and please Him, or we can use it in ways that do not honor Him.

However, we need to see that true riches do not necessarily mean a big bank account or gigantic home with six luxury cars in front.

There are other ways that God can make us rich that matter even more than how much money we have.

For example, I have five children who I love intensely. Because I value their character and relationship with God more than anything, I feel like a rich, rich man that my three oldest girls (at this writing the two youngest are 14 year old twins) are serving God whole-heartedly and demonstrating truly Godly character. I wouldn't trade those "riches" for a million dollars!

When I counsel couples that are struggling in their marriage and can hardly stand each other I feel like a rich man to be married to Gloria, the woman I love, and have peace in our home. God promises His people—and if you are a Christian, that includes you—in Deuteronomy, "(I) will grant you *abundant* prosperity".

He wants to meet our needs (*Phil. 4:19*), fulfill our desires (*Psa. 37:4*), *and* give us abundance. If we cooperate with His plans for our financial life, then we should believe for and look for His abundant blessing—more than enough, more than is normal. But remember, it is not just about money, it's about blessings—God's favor on your life.

We should ask God and believe Him for abundant favor on our families, on our jobs, paying off our debts, everything we put our hands to. God does not want you to just get by, so ask Him for more. What do you need right now? If you are obeying Him by being generous in giving, then ask and believe for His abundance.

You will be amazed at what He does.

Day 31: Action Steps

1. What is the greatest blessing that God has put into your life? _____

   Spend a moment and simply thank Him for it.

2. What do you need from God right now? _____
   Take some time and ask Him for it. Even if you are not sure God exists, ask Him, do what He tells you to do and see what He does.

Day 32:

Wise Wealth Part II

He who gathers money little by little makes it grow.
Proverbs 13:11 (NIV)

*H*ere is a good piece of wisdom for you; "Don't try to get rich too quick."

We all are attracted to the latest something-for-almost-nothing scheme. Maybe it's the widow of the millionaire in Africa that picked you out of millions of Americans to manage her fortune, and, of course, keep a big chunk. It may be the chain letter that promises incredible returns if you send in your hundred bucks to the guy on top of the list and add your name to the bottom, or the hot stock that no one else knows about that is about to go through the roof.

The slow and tedious work of managing the money that God has entrusted into our care is not much fun, but Proverbs 21:5 gives us great warning; "shortcuts lead to poverty."

We all want to believe that there is an easier way to make money. This feeling is what every scam artist relies upon. The truth is, God only lends us the money that we have and requires that we invest it with care.

We've already talked about giving and tithing, but what do you do with the rest? We invest it wisely and let it build slowly. A good, honest financial adviser will let you know how to balance risk and potential return so that you are building safely and wisely.

We need to resist the urge to become impatient. Competent investment counselors will tell you that it is their client's lack of patience that, very often, leads them to rash decisions and loss.

Proverbs 28:20 warns, "The person who wants to get rich quick will only get into trouble."

Get Smart

In the great Internet stock bubble of the 90's, the people who did the best where those who stayed away from the speculative, get-rich-quick start ups and patiently stuck with a long term plan for slow but steady growth.

It seems Solomon knew what he was talking about.

Proverbs 27:23-24a advises; "Know the state of your flocks, and put your heart into caring for your herds, for riches don't last forever". Most of us do not have flocks or herds, so Solomon might say to us, "Balance your checkbook regularly and make sure you know how your 401K is doing. Your money won't take care of itself if you are not watching it."

Some people simply don't want to think about financial matters, but God has entrusted this money into our care and we must take care of it. "Put your heart into it", we are advised.

It's okay to let a qualified, credentialed professional help with the management of our funds, but we should learn enough to know how to read the reports and understand the state of our finances.

One Wednesday night I was in charge of a small discussion group and, as I often did, I asked; "Is there anyone who has had something good in their life that they would like to share?"

One young man, probably in his mid 30's raised his hand.

He told us about how he was concerned about paying some bills and while he was thinking about this, he went to get something from a dresser drawer. There, he said, he found a checkbook for an account he forgot he had. In it was $10,000. He forgot about a $10,000 bank account! There was someone who needed to be more aware of his finances.

How about you? Right now, review your approach to investing God's money.

Do you know where you are financially? If not, find out! Then read up on to discover what you need to know to be a wise steward of what you have been given—no matter how small or large.

Day 32: Action Steps

1. Is there any place in your life where you are expecting
   to "get rich quick"? _____
   Are you putting your finances at risk by doing so? _____

2. Do you know the current state of your finances (bank
   accounts, 401K, IRA etc.)? _____
   If not, what do you need to do to find out? _____
   When will you take this step? _____

Day 33:

Dumb Debt

The borrower is slave to the lender.
Proverbs 22:7 TNIV

In January of 2003 NPR reported, *"American consumers now owe about $1.7 trillion in credit card and other debts -- an amount roughly equal to the gross national product of England and Russia combined."*

It has only gotten worse since then. Many reading this book are probably carrying balances on their credit cards from month to month and often paying high interest rates. If that is you, you need to get yourself out of debt.

While it is always good to be debt free, there are times when debt is more understandable than others. One is if you are in debt for something that has more value than what is owed on it, like a reasonably priced car. Another is buying a home rather than renting. You can always sell the asset and pay off the loan.

Unsecured, high interest credit card debt is not a wise idea.

What is it about debt that makes it so unwise?

When we are in debt, we are a slave to the lender (as it says in the verse above). How much better to be free to spend our money on our families' real needs or on helping others rather than on interest. When we are in debt our first obligation is to the lender. Only after we have satisfied them can we ask what we can do with what is left over.

Beyond that, God wants us to be free from anxiety. It is hard to be at peace when we are not even sure the bill that is coming in the mail can be paid. We can get especially anxious when get behind and the creditors are calling and the nasty letters are coming. That is simply not what God wants for us.

Additionally, God wants us to learn to be dependent on Him, not our credit card, for provision. When we start getting into the habit of spending on credit, we stop going to God to ask for His help and start relying on the almighty Visa instead.

So, if you find yourself in debt and you don't want to be a slave to the credit card companies anymore, what do you do?

First, get honest about what you owe. Make a complete list of who you owe money to listing the balance due on each loan and the interest rate you are paying.

Secondly, come to God in prayer. Repent for your lack of good stewardship with His money and make a commitment to Him to change your way of doing things. Ask Him to help you keep those commitments and to provide what you will need to get free.

If you are married, make sure your spouse is part of this.

Thirdly, cut up your credit cards. Get rid of them and don't get anymore.

Fourth, as God provides extra income for you, be disciplined to use it to pay off your debts—the highest interest rate first. When you have one card paid off, add that payment to the next one on the list.

Fifth, keep it up. Daily ask God for His help. It is a good idea, every week or two, to have a "family meeting" with your spouse to review your commitments and progress.

Here is how one wise woman, Georgia did it;

> *I paid off 30k in credit card debt and personal loans in 12 months. I changed my expectations, and decided my life-style should be based in financial reality. I decided that paying down debt was my number one priority. I started reading anything I could find on how to live frugally. I implemented numerous cost cutting ideas, such as using a price book and coupons, bundling services, and shopping for better insurance rates. I started making dinner at home, I canceled all memberships and magazine subscriptions. Anything and everything to reduce fixed monthly expenses.*

On top of that, I opened a second bank account. I pay all the household bills from one account using automatic bill pay. The second account I deposit a set amount of money for my "living expenses." When it's gone, spending is over. Any and all money left over goes to pay off debt. For me the way to succeed was to change material expectations and make debt reduction a priority.

God wants us to be free and it can be done. Let's make a commitment to finding freedom in this essential area.

Day 33: Action Steps

1. How much do you owe on credit cards? _____
   If you don't know, you need to find out.

2. If you are carrying a balance, what is your plan for paying them off?_____What are you willing to do without in order to be free from the bondage of debt?
   _____

Day 34:

Grubby Greed

A greedy person tries to get rich quick,
but it only leads to poverty.
Proverbs 28:22 (NLT)

*I*n the movie <u>Wall Street </u>the lead character Gordon Gekko famously says, "Greed, for the lack of a better term, is good."

While Mr. Gekko may see its positive side and many in our world are driven by it, (although few will admit it) God is not in favor of greed. In His word (I Corinthians 6:10) He says that the greedy are not even going to make it into heaven!

If "greed" is so bad, we had better define what it is!

It is, as the bible talks about it, an insatiable desire to always have more, to have what someone else has, no matter what it takes—even if you have to take it from them. It is the opposite of a contented, generous heart.

It is an attitude that looks out for one's own good to the detriment of others.In the book of Proverbs alone we are warned that greed will keep us from true satisfaction, from giving to others (21:25-26), that it causes fighting (28:25), robs us of the joy of life (1:19), ensnares us in a trap (11:6) and greedy people make trouble for their family (15:27).

Adam Smith suggested that greed was the only thing that would motivate people to work. God has other ideas. As His followers we don't need greed as our motivation to work. We work because, as we saw earlier, God doesn't want us to be lazy and we want to have enough to give generously to others.

Proverbs 21:25-26 says it so well; "The desires of lazy people will be their ruin, for their hands refuse to work. They are always greedy for more, while the godly love to give!" Those who love God work to give!

Do you struggle with greed? Here are a few questions to check yourself out with;

How content are you with what God has given you?

How often do you deal with jealousy over what others have, the vacations they take or the money they have in the bank? Interestingly, it is possible to be greedy even without having a lot of money. My friend Jack is that kind of guy.

If greed is always feeling like you just need "just a little bit more", then Jack is greedy. He has a great business that provides for him and his family and serves the community, but he always has the feeling that it needs to do just a little bit better, that it needs to bring in just a little bit more money.

What does that mean for Jack? That he has to work "just a little bit more." This now means that he works, nearly every week, 60 or 70 hours.

As his friend, I have challenged him time after time that his over focus on his business is detrimental to his health, his friendships but, most importantly to his wife and family. Still, Jack can't stop trying to do "just a little more" and, frankly, it is slowly killing him. Greed is draining the life out of my dear friend.

Do you often feel like you can't be happy until you have "just a little bit more"? If you find yourself dealing with this green eyed monster, here are three things you can do;

First, give! Nothing kills greed faster than giving to others. You can't have an open hand and clenched fist at the same time.

Second, cultivate an attitude of thankfulness for everything you have. Write it down in a list and thank God regularly for it.

Third, watch your thoughts and actions. If you start feeling resentful when someone else gets something new, something you wanted, ask God to forgive you and let Him change your heart.

Fourth, set your heart on the things of God. Spend more time with Him in His Word and prayer. Begin to value more deeply the things you can't buy but have immense, eternal value; His presence and love,

His work in your life and through you.

Finally, set limits on your time. Decide how much time you need to spend on creating wealth for your family and when that time is up, STOP! Don't let greed make you a workaholic.

These steps will help you stamp greed out of your life before it gets a chance to destroy you.

Day 34: Action Steps

1. Review the "check yourself out" questions that start on the bottom of page 111. Give yourself a score 1 to 10 on how greedy your are (1=no greed, 10=I have to have a little more all the time) _____

2. If your scored 5 or above on any of the questions, which of the actions steps do you need to work on?_____
   What is your first step? _____

Section 6

SMART
HEART

Day 35:

The Heart of the Issue

My son, give me your heart,
And let your eyes observe my ways.
Proverbs 23:26 (RSV)

Since this last section deals with our heart, it is probably best to begin with a definition.

What is the "heart"? We use that word often, but we sometimes understand it too little.

When the book of Proverbs uses this word, it is referring to who we are inside, the real us. It's what we would call our soul. It can be described as the seat of our emotions, our mind and conscience. It is the very center of who we are, the true person without anything disguised or obscured.

God's Word makes it clear that people see us for who we are on the outside, but God sees us and rewards us for who we are in our hearts. A wise heart, then, begins by realizing that you can't hide anything from God.

I counseled with Henry many years ago. It was, frankly, a very frustrating experience. Henry kept having problems in his marriage and with his family. He was mean and abusive to them and he blamed it on his job and how stressful it was.

It seemed reasonable that this high stress occupation was creating some real problems for this man. So we worked on his stress level. We talked about what happened at work and how to relate to it in a more healthy way.

We talked about how to find joy and refreshment in his life. I encouraged him to commit to physical exercise in order to relieve some of the pressure.

Nothing seemed to work.

It was not until many months later that I discovered the real problem. Henry revealed to his wife and family that he was having a homosexual affair. Now, everything made sense. No wonder he was under such pressure and no wonder nothing I suggested was doing any good.

The problem was, Henry was not being honest about what was in his heart.

Unless and until the heart issue was uncovered and dealt with, he was never going to be effective in dealing with his actions in his family and marriage. He had a heart problem and I didn't even know it.

Never forget, no one else may know but God knows your heart. If it is not right, don't try to hide it.

Ask Him to help you change who you really are.

Day 35: Action Steps

1. Are there any heart issues you are trying to hide, even from God? _____

2. Are you willing to let Him deal with it? _____
   If so, ask for Him to.

Day 36:

The Makings of A Wise Heart

My child, listen and be wise.
Keep your heart on the right course.
Proverbs 23:19 (NLT)

As we work to understand what a wise heart is like, the third chapter of Proverbs is a great place to start.

First it tells us, "Good friend, don't forget all I've taught you; take to heart my commands."

The first characteristic of a wise heart is that it holds on to what it learns and internalizes those lessons.

How many times have we caused problems for ourselves because we learned something important, but then forgot it at the crucial moment?

A wise heart is a retaining heart—one that works to remind itself about truth. We all forget, we all have to be reminded.

I hope that during these 40 days you have been reading the book of Proverbs as well as this book. If you haven't you should start. You may forget what is written in this book, but choose to make it a habit to come back time after time to Proverbs so that you don't forget what it says about living life in a wise way.

It promises you that if you do, it will "help you live a long, long time, a long life lived full and well."

Next we see in Proverbs 3, "Don't lose your grip on love and loyalty. Tie them around your neck; carve their initials on your heart."

We are called to be those who love and don't stop loving easily. There is a scarcity of both in our world. It is hard to find someone who loves with a truly committed heart to start with, and it is even harder to find someone who will stay committed to their relationships even when times get tough.

That is the kind of heart that God honors and rewards. In fact, this scripture makes promises to those with that kind of heart, "God and people will like you and consider you a success." That is a blessing we would all like to have.

My friend Jim is this kind of man.

The picture I have of Jim is of him walking up to greet me, pushing his wife in a wheelchair. His wife, Carolyn, had a strange set of symptoms. She tripped and hurt her ankle but as time went by, the ankle didn't get better, it got worse. She was walking with a cane, later a walker and then a wheelchair.

After many instances of misdiagnosis, we learned that she had Lou Gehrigs disease, ALS.

Over the next few months I watched with great sadness as her physical body slipped gradually but continually into paralysis. In the last stages, she was bed ridden and had to be taken care of 24 hours a day.

Not too many weeks later, she began to lose her ability to breath and, with the family gathered around, she left this life and entered the next.

What so impressed me, was Jim's absolute commitment to her. As the months wore on and her needs increased, he would step up without complaint and do whatever needed to be done.

Jim stayed committed to Carolyn even when it wasn't convenient. Even when it cost him dearly in time and treasure. He is an example of a man with the kind of heart God wants us to have.

Finally in Proverbs 3 we read, "With all your heart you must trust the LORD and not your own judgment. Always let Him lead you."

A wise heart is one who trusts God for direction in life.

By contrast, a person with an unwise heart decides that they know more than God and can do whatever seems right to them. That is dangerous—in fact, it will destroy your life. God made you and knows what is best, even when it doesn't "feel" like it. A wise heart knows that.

It may "feel" right to lie or cheat or to get involved sexually outside of marriage, but it is not right and it will destroy you.

On the other hand, if we listen and trust what He says we are promised, "He will clear the road for you to follow."

If with a wise heart you listen to what God tells you, He will give you direction and make things work out for your best as you follow it. A wise heart knows that it is always the right thing to do to trust God and recognizes that there are blessings that come from it.

Day 36: Action Steps

1. You may not want to write this down but consider how loyal your really are to the most important relationships in your life (your spouse, your best friend)? Are you committed to never losing sight of "love and faithfulness"?

2. Is there any area in your life where you are not letting God direct you?_____If there is, take a moment right now to turn it over to Him and start trusting and obeying His direction.

Day 37:

The Results of A Wise Heart

For the happy heart, life is a continual feast.
Proverbs 15:15b (NLT)

What happens when we have the right kind of heart?

In the verse above, the word translated "happy" really means nothing more than "good" or "right". In other words, if our hearts are good and right, then our lives will be a party—pleasant and enjoyable.

There are two reasons that this is true.

First, when are hearts are right, when we are making good, wise godly choices, we don't have to deal with guilt, shame and regret. It is those things that weigh us down, keep us up at night and wake us up in the morning filled with anxiety. But also, when we are living from good and right hearts, our lives will be blessed!

God will make sure that "life is a continual feast." He will give you something to celebrate.

Proverbs 14:30 tells us, "A heart at peace gives life to the body, but envy rots the bones." Later in the Bible, Paul the Apostle teaches his young student Timothy that, "Godliness with contentment is great gain."

In other words, as this verse points out, when we have a heart that is content instead of jealous of what others have, we are far better off. Envy causes us to miss out on enjoying what we do have simply because someone else has more.

If we let envy creep into your heart, realize that it will be corrosive to our insides. It will make us unhappy and resentful, and can even literally cause disease in our bodies ("envy rots the bones").

Get Smart

This simple story illustrates the right kind of heart so well:

A businessman was at the pier of a small coastal Mexican village when a small boat with just one fisherman docked. Inside the small boat were several large yellowfin tuna.

The businessman complimented the Mexican on the quality of his fish and asked how long it took to catch them. The Mexican replied only a little while.

The businessman then asked why he didn't stay out longer and catch more fish?

The Mexican said he had enough to support his family's immediate needs. The businessman then asked, but what do you do with the rest of your time?

The Mexican fisherman said, "I sleep late, fish a little, play with my children, take a siesta with my wife, Maria, stroll into the village each evening where I sip wine and play guitar with my amigos; I have a full and busy life, señor."

The businessman scoffed, "I am a Harvard MBA and I could help you. You should spend more time fishing and with the proceeds buy a bigger boat.

With the proceeds from the bigger boat you could buy several boats; eventually you would have a fleet of fishing boats. Instead of selling your catch to a middleman, you would sell directly to the processor and eventually open your own cannery.

You would control the product, processing and distribution. You would need to leave this small coastal fishing village and move to Mexico City, then LA and eventually New York City where you would run your expanding enterprise."

The Mexican fisherman asked, "But señor, how long will this all take?" To which the businessman replied, "15-20 years." "But what then, señor?" The businessman laughed and said, "That's the best part! When the time is right you would announce an IPO and sell your company stock to the public and become very rich. You would make millions."

"Millions, señor? Then what?" The businessman said, "Then you would retire. Move to a small coastal fishing village where you would sleep late, fish a little, play with your kids, take a siesta with your wife, stroll to the village in the evenings where you could sip wine and play your guitar with your amigos."

The fisherman, still smiling, looked up and said, "Isn't that what I'm doing right now?"

Secondly, the heart described here is a healthy heart, a sound, healed up heart. Often what makes us jealous or envious of what others have is an emotional wound in our own hearts. We don't feel able to measure up to others; that somehow we are lacking.

Our heart tells us that maybe if we just had what they have; the clothes, the house, the money, the cars, the relationships, the physical looks, then we would feel okay.

The truth is only God, not stuff, can bring about soundness and healing in our hearts. A person with a wounded, envious heart, no matter how much they have, will always feel like they are less than or lacking.

If you suffer like this in your own heart, don't try to fill the gap with stuff. Ask God to heal you and make you able to realize that you are already more than enough (*because you are*), and that you already have all that you need. The result is that you can be at peace, and your physical health could even improve ("gives life to the body").

As you hear what a wise heart is like and the results of it, you can either learn, change, grow and benefit; or you can ignore it and miss out on what you could receive.

In fact, Proverbs 18:15 says; "Wise men and women are always learning, always listening for fresh insights."

Choose to have a heart that looks for the truth, and when you find it, apply it to your life. Don't miss out on a chance to have a better and more fulfilling life!

Day 37: Action Steps

1. Is there any place of disobedience to God that is weighing your heart down?_____If so, confess it and ask Him to give you the grace to change.

2. Be honest. If every *thing* that you have was taken from you would you still feel like you are a person of value and worth? _____
   Do you need *stuff* to feel OK? _____

   If so, ask God to show you how valuable you are and heal up that place in your heart.

Day 38:

Our Dangerous Heart

Keep your heart with all diligence,
For out of it spring the issues of life.
Proverbs 4:23 (NKJV)

Our hearts are dangerous things because they set the course of our lives. After watching the final episode of Star Wars I recognized that what turned Anakin to evil was that his heart was seduced by fear and the lust for power. As his heart went, so did the course of his life.

If we must "keep our hearts", what is it that we must watch for?

Most often our hearts are drawn away by our affections, the things we have come to love the very most.

Sometimes those affections are unhealthy and dangerous for us. That is why we can not blindly follow the Disney motto: "follow your heart" because sometimes our hearts are going in the wrong direction.

Proverbs 5 depicts the person who has been led down the wrong path by an out of control heart. "And you mourn at last, when your flesh and your body are consumed, and say: 'How I have hated instruction, and my heart despised correction!'" (vs. 11-12)

It didn't take me too long to discover that if there was one thing that Jerry loved, it was alcohol.

He had had his first beer at six years old and has struggled with drinking ever sense. He knew that it wasn't good for his family. He knew that it was destroying his health but he also loved the taste and smell of it and, especially, how it made him feel.

I really tried to help him; I read books with him, counseled and encouraged him but there was always one barrier that I could not overcome.

Alcohol had Jerry's heart and he would not let it go.

I saw him a few days ago. He was on a new treatment for one of his many physical aliments. Because of the drug he was on, drinking made him very ill. Perhaps God is using this to wrench his heart free from this fatal attachment.

A dangerous heart, a destructive heart is one that refuses to be corrected, that hates to be told what to do. The world around us tells us to be independent, to believe that we don't need anyone's advice or help.

Yet, if we follow that course and allow our hearts to be filled with that kind of pride, it will bring us to destruction.

In fact Proverbs 18:12 says, "Before destruction the heart of a man is haughty, and before honor is humility."

A heart that refuses correction is a dangerous heart.

Another kind of dangerous heart is what Proverbs calls a twisted heart. Proverbs 11:20 is very straightforward on this; "The Lord hates people with twisted hearts, but he delights in those who have integrity."

The word "twisted" is variously translated "perverse", "crooked", "deceitful", even "sneaky". It refers to a heart that wants to go one direction, towards what is wrong and bad, but desires to have everyone think that they are doing the right thing. That kind of heart is trouble.

This verse tells us that God "hates" that kind of person. He would rather that we would have the guts to admit that we are doing what we want to, even if it is wrong, than to pretend to be doing right and, at the same time, covering up our sin.

Sometimes our hearts are so twisted that we have convinced ourselves that the evil in our lives is okay. In fact, there will be plenty of people around us who are willing to tell us that we are doing just fine.

The way to untwist our hearts is to be willing to admit to ourselves, and perhaps to a godly person we trust, that what we are doing is wrong. The reason God hates a twisted heart is because that kind of heart will not seek the help it needs to change.

If you are doing the wrong thing and trying to hide it, deny it or justify it, let Him untwist your heart. Confess what you are doing and seek His help to change.

It is the only way to make a dangerous heart safe again.

Day 38: Action Steps

1. Does your heart have a fatal attraction? Is there something like alcohol, drugs, pornography an illicit relationship or even rage that your heart stubbornly refuses to give up_____? Will you give it to God and do whatever you need to do to get free? _____

2. Are you brave enough to pray this prayer?

"Dear God, if there is anything in my heart that you say is wrong and I have justified, please show me and show me how you want to remove it."

Day 39:

The Results of A Heart Gone Astray

The backslider in heart will be filled with the fruit of his ways.
Proverbs 14:14 (ESV)

The simple truth is this; you will reap what you sow.

If you sow from a bad heart—wrong desires, motivations and affections, you will get bad results. Count on it!

Proverbs 16:5 warns us, "Everyone proud in heart is an abomination to the Lord".

The proud in heart are those who believe that they alone are responsible for the successes in their lives. They consider that the things they have and positions they fill are purely a result of their own initiative and self-reliance.

Why does God hate the proud heart? Because it takes credit for things God has made happen. How do you feel when others take credit for what you have done?

Do you get angry? So does God.

Secondly, God hates our pride because it puts us above others in our own minds, believing we should be first and most important. Our pride argues against the truth that God has made us all equal in value, and attempts to make sure *its* needs are met first and most often.

Pride has no place for submission to another's concerns or putting them first.

The scripture above promises that such a heart will be punished. The self-reliance of pride brings destruction. This kind of pride and self centeredness is intensely damaging to the most important relationships in our lives; with our family and friends, and it destroys our intimacy with God.

If you want to live under the blessing of God, learn to have a humble heart—one that recognizes its absolute need for God's help and provision. Practice the humility of putting others first and valuing others as God does.

If you have that kind of heart, God has promised you His blessing.

We started this chapter with Proverbs 14:14 which instructs us, "The backslider in heart will be filled with the fruit of his ways."

There seems to be very little that possesses more power over our actions than our old habits of mind, and heart that we are attempting to leave behind us. Each day we are faced with the test; will we continue in our path to growth and maturity, or turn back and take the easy way?

We need to remind our hearts at the moment of decision that there was a reason we changed. The old ways were not working. They were, in fact, destructive to our life and relationships. As this scripture warns, to go back is to reap the consequences all over again.

Remember this; the crop we reap is worse the second time around. The habits start up faster and grab us harder. The gap between sowing the bad seed and getting bad harvest is smaller.

If there was one person who knew better than to go back, it was my friend Brent. He had begun to spend way too much time with another woman besides his wife. His heart was being ensnared by this relationship. Fortunately for him, the relationship came to light and, with the help of his close friends, he got out before it went too far.

Unfortunately, the story doesn't end there. Months later my friend Brent secretly started spending time with this same woman again. The relationship came on faster and stronger than before.

By the time it came to light he lost his job, his reputation and nearly lost his marriage.

If you are tempted to go back to the things God has rescued you out of, realize what is at stake and ask Him, plead with Him, for His help. It's not too late, but now is the time to decide to step forward into blessing instead of backward into danger.

Now is the time to get your heart on the right track.

Day 39: Action Steps

1. Do you have a prideful heart? Do you take credit for things that God has done for you?_____Take a moment to ask Him to forgive you and give you the humility we all need.

2. Is there an old habit of life that is sneaking up on your heart? Something you thought you had conquered but now is slipping back into your life? If so, what is it? _____ Which of your friends can you confess to and get them to help you get it out of your life once and for all?

   _____

Day 40:

God and Your Heart

Fire tests the purity of silver and gold,
but the Lord tests the heart.
Proverbs 17:3 (NLT)

There are many ways that God tests our hearts.

As another Proverb points out, "People may think they are doing what is right, but the Lord examines the heart."

We may be able to fool others, we may even be able to fool ourselves for a time, but God knows our real motivations. Part of His testing of our hearts is to make these motivations clear to us.

For example, we may believe that we are serving others from the highest of motives, that our only reason for service is to care for people and see their needs met.

Then comes a period of time when we are tested by criticism of the very way we serve. Those judging our service don't even see the sacrifices we have made, and even suggest that we're doing it for our own good instead of for those we love and freely serve.

Our reaction to this opposition reveals our true heart.

If we react in anger or by simply giving up, then we have to face what is really in our hearts. We were really serving for what we could get instead of what we could give. We were serving to please people instead of God.

God uses others' opposition and criticism to reveal our hearts. Other times He uses failure or success to test us. If we succeed, we are tempted to be filled with pride, which, as we saw yesterday, is a very dangerous thing.

Success in itself does not create pride, it simply reveals what is already there. It exposes a heart that was convinced all along that success or failure was entirely in its own hands--a heart that is self-reliant instead of God reliant.

When we succeed, others will be quick to tell us how great, and smart, able and insightful we are. The danger is that we will believe what they tell us! If there is any tendency to think that we are better than others, that we should be treated with extraordinary deference and respect, that tendency will come into full bloom when we have others telling us of our greatness. It is then that we will pass or fail the test of success.

Failure tests us in other ways. Certainly, when we fail, it's right for us to assess our own responsibility for what happened—things that we knew we should have done, or refrained from doing.

Yet, to believe that our failure is entirely in our own hands and of our own doing, that we are responsible for the uncontrollable, is to reveal a different kind of prideful heart. A heart willing to assume powers that only God possesses.

Failure reveals a heart that will either get up, get going again and trust God to help us learn and do better in the next effort, or a heart that will harbor bitterness towards God, give up and quit trying.

The trust in God or willingness to blame Him was always there. The test of failure simply reveals it.

I was blessed (or cursed) with a lot of success early in my life as a Pastor. When I was in my early 20's I was asked to speak each Sunday night to a congregation that grew from 450 to more than 800. I had people telling me that I was gifted and talented. I once was mowing my front lawn when a car came to a screeching halt in the street next to me. The person asked with obvious excitement: "Are you Randy Sanford?" I assured them that it was me. Evidently their sister had heard me speak at one of my regular Sunday night services because she exclaimed, "My sister thinks you are the best thing since sliced bread."

Pretty heady stuff for young man just a year or two out of Bible College and, sadly, it did go to my head. I began to think that I was pretty important and quite gifted. I did not pass the pride test.

I sometimes believe that God has spent the rest of my life freeing me of that notion. Later in my life trying to start a church with only moderate success and then trying to grow a large church with very little success, I came to understand the other side of the equation. If I am responsible for my own success, I am also responsible for my own failures.

God has taught me over the last thirty years of working for Him in ministry, that the biggest challenge I face is not whether I succeed or fail but it is the heart test. In good times or bad will I hold on to a humble heart, reliant on Him for my value and worth and dependent on him no matter what happens.

Frankly sometimes I have passed this heart test and sometimes I have failed, but at this point in my life I can truthfully say that my life, my value and my future are completely in His hands. I have learned the hard way, to be fully content in that position.

When you face these trials then, you ought to be thankful. You may not even be aware of what is in your own heart. Whatever these challenges in your life reveal about your heart, know this; if it is needed, God desires to cleanse, renew and change you.

Be thankful that God cares enough to give you this revelation, even if it is hard to face, and then ask Him, humbly, to bring the change that is needed.

Day 40: Action Steps

1. How has God tested your heart? _____

   _____

2. Did you pass or fail?_____If you failed, what do you need
   to do now so you can pass next time? _____

   _____

Get Smart

HANG ON TO IT!

"I knew better than that!" Have you ever said this?

Notice the tense of the word "knew".

It reveals something very important. Even when we have set ourselves to study and understand wisdom, it can be stolen away. We can forget what we "knew".

In the parable of the sower that Jesus tells, the seed that represents His wise words, falls on the hard ground and is eaten by the birds. It is never allowed to make a difference in the way the person lives their life. This gives us a clue to one way we can preserve what we have gained these last 40 days. Proverbs 4:21 admonishes us to "let them (*the author's words*) penetrate deep within your heart". It is not enough to know what Proverbs says, we must allow the penetration to happen by living it out!

It is when it becomes part of the basic way we look at life, conduct ourselves and make our decisions, that these truths can be said to be *in* our hearts. Once they are fully there they are hard to lose.

In Proverbs 4 we are instructed in regards to the truths of this book, "do not forget my words or swerve from them. Do not forsake wisdom, and she will protect you; love her, and she will watch over you."

There are two ways to put this admonishment into practice. First, make it a habit to memorize some of these Proverbs. If you do so, you will have them when you need them most.

Secondly, revisit the book regularly. Many people have made it a habit to read one chapter of Proverbs each day besides their regular Bible reading. Since there are 31 chapters in the book and 31 days in

each month, it is easy to read the "chapter for the day." Whatever day of the month it is, turn to that chapter and read it. It is a great habit to form.

However you go about it just remember the importance of retaining what you have learned these last 40 days.

The truths of the book of Proverbs are too important to allow to slip away. If you retain them, and live them, you are promised to be blessed!

STEPS TO BEGINNING A RELATIONSHIP WITH GOD

In the first section we saw how wisdom begins with the "fear of God". This is not referring to being afraid of God's punishment, but a fear that shows itself in respect for His greatness and majesty.

God wants to have a relationship with you. He loves you and wants to be close to you. What separates you from Him is a problem we all contend with—our sin. We have all done things that we knew were wrong. No one can say that they are as holy as God.

The problem is, God only can have holy people near Him. So, how do you deal with the sin issue so that you and God can have a relationship?

The good news is that Jesus, God's Son came down to earth, lived a perfect life, died and rose again for one reason, so that you can be close to God.

Someone had to pay the penalty for your sins. God says, "the wages (*the consequences*) of sin is death."

Because God loved you so much, He sent His Son to die in your place.

How should you respond? How do you get right with God?

Simply follow these steps;

- ◆ **Confess your sins.** The Bible tells us that if we confess what we have done wrong, God will forgive us. Don't worry that you can't remember them all. Confess what you can remember and when God brings more to your mind, confess those.

- ◆ **Repent.** To repent means nothing more than turning around and going the other way. It is telling God that you want to live life His way from now on.

- **Believe.** Take it as the truth that Jesus died for you and that when He rose from the dead opened the way to come to God our Father.

- **Accept.** Right now say this, or something like it, to God. He's listening to everything you have to say;

  "Dear God, thank you that you love me enough to send Jesus to die for my sins. I accept Him as my savior and ask you to come into my life. God I want to get to know you. I want to live for you. Please forgive me and accept me as your child."

- **Tell.** Now tell your Christian friends what you have just done and tell others who don't know Jesus how to get to know Him.

Congratulations!

You have just taken the most important step you will ever take!

If you want to grow then get a Bible and start reading. Find a church that teaches the Bible and get involved with it. Develop friendships with Christians and let them help you grow.

I would love to hear from you about taking this step, so write me at randall@vision2lead.coach and we'll get you some more help in your walk with God.

If you have any other questions, feel free to email me as well.

20367898R00080